Philippians/Colossians
Experiencing the Joy of Knowing Christ

Bruce BICKEL
&
Stan JANTZ

HARVEST HOUSE PUBLISHERS

EUGENE, OREGON

Cover by Left Coast Design, Portland, Oregon

Cover photo by Steve Terrill Photography; www.terrillphoto.com

Harvest House Publishers, Inc., is the exclusive licensee of the trademark CHRISTIANITY 101.

PHILIPPIANS/COLOSSIANS: EXPERIENCING THE JOY OF KNOWING CHRIST
Copyright © 2004 by Bruce Bickel and Stan Jantz
Published by Harvest House Publishers
Eugene, Oregon 97402
www.harvesthousepublishers.com

Library of Congress Cataloging-in-Publication Data

Bickel, Bruce, 1952–
    Philippians/Colossians : experiencing the joy of knowing Christ / Bruce Bickel and Stan Jantz.
        p. cm. — (Christianity 101)
    ISBN 0-7369-0939-7 (pbk.)
    1. Bible. N.T. Philippians—Criticism, interpretation, etc. 2. Bible. N.T. Colossians—Criticism, interpretation, etc. I. Jantz, Stan, 1952– II. Title. III. Series.
    BS2705.52.B53 2004
    227'.607—dc22

                                                                2003023092

Printed in the United States of America

  04   05   06   07   08   09   10   11   / DP-MS /   10   9   8   7   6   5   4   3   2   1

Contents

A Note from the Authors

*W*e know this is a Bible study on Philippians and Colossians, but we feel compelled to start off with a verse from the Gospel of John. It doesn't rank up there in fame and notoriety with John 3:16, but it is pretty well known (at least with Christians). What makes this verse so intriguing is that Christians believe it (because Jesus said it), but they often struggle to find proof of it. The verse follows the "I am the vine and you are the branches" lecture that Jesus gave to His disciples:

> *I have told you this so that you will be filled with my joy. Yes, your joy will overflow* (John 15:11).

Wow! What a statement. What a promise. Isn't that exactly what all of us want? In a world with circumstances that knock us about, we need a spirit of joy just to get us through most days. Let's face it. Life doesn't play out like a Hallmark commercial, with sweet sentiments permeating the environment. Nope—in real life we have financial worries, relational problems, physical challenges, emotional stress, and a slew of seemingly insurmountable obstacles facing us.

And being a Christian doesn't automatically make things any easier. In fact, Christianity often complicates our lives. Being Christlike in a pagan culture only adds to the tension. We're trying to be salt and light in a culture that prefers the darkness and despises our opinions about society's need to change its beliefs and lifestyles.

Most of us are in desperate need of the joy Christ promised. We've never experienced overflowing joy. We'd be pleased if we could just get a trickle of it. Most Christians know that experiencing a soul-satisfying joy must be possible. You've got no doubt because Jesus promised it to the disciples—and to you. Your only problem is figuring out how to take advantage of what Jesus promised.

Well, we've got good news and great news for you. The good news is that you aren't the only one to struggle with this quandary. And that leads us to the great news. Because so many of the first-century Christians needed to experience Christ's joy in their lives (as is often the case when you are being thrown to the lions), the apostle Paul frequently wrote about this subject. Paul's premise is that life-fulfilling joy comes from knowing and understanding Christ and appreciating our relationship with Him. Those are the themes that you'll find in Philippians and Colossians.

Two Books in One

You'll find Philippians and Colossians side-by-side in your Bible, but that is not why we have included them together in this single Bible study. Although these letters were written to different audiences, they share the same author and have overlapping themes. Without giving away the punch line, we'll tell you now that Philippians deals more with the subject of *joy,* and Colossians focuses more on *knowing Christ.* But these themes are interrelated and interdependent.

Studying Philippians without Colossians would leave you with an appreciation for the effects of joy, but you might fall a little short on knowing how it is produced in your own life. Conversely, understanding Colossians might leave you high on theological doctrine but dry on the experiential side. So we applaud your decision to study these two books of the Bible at the same time.

The first seven chapters of this book will guide you through Philippians. Chapter 1 will give you an overview; chapters 2–7 will dissect Philippians on a passage-by-passage basis. Then we'll move to Colossians with the same format. Chapter 8 will provide you with the big picture of Colossians, and chapters 9–13 will take you to a ground-level study of the verses.

Christianity 101 Series

This Bible study is part of the Christianity 101 series that includes other Bible studies and resource books (such as *Knowing God 101* and *Creation and Evolution 101).* All of these books are designed to present the truth about God in a manner that is correct, clear, and casual. We intend the Bible studies to give you additional background information (the kind you'll find in a commentary, only not so technical) along with questions that encourage you to apply what you have studied to your individual life circumstances.

As a participant in this Bible study, you're invited to log onto www.Christianity101online.com. There you will find additional resources, information, and study questions that may be helpful in your study of Philippians and Colossians. The website has pages for each of the books in the Christianity 101 series. You can also use the website to e-mail to us any questions you have about what you have studied. Look at the end of this book for more information about these online features.

You (and Others If You Wish)

We've designed this Bible study for individuals as well as groups, so you can work through this book as part of a daily devotional plan or as part of a weekly group. The questions at the end of each chapter are designed for personal reflections as well as group discussion.

We don't usually print the verses that are being discussed. That is what your Bible is for. We suggest that you read the Bible passage first and then read through the chapter in this book. Then, reread the Bible passage for a second time. (These are short passages we're talking about, so you'll still have time for eating and sleeping.) We think you'll be surprised how much better you understand that passage when you read it for a second time.

Joy from Knowing

As you might expect, we've been praying a lot as we write this book. We've been asking that God will guide our words as we try to clearly communicate the tremendous connection between *knowing God* and *experiencing joy* that Paul explains in Colossians and Philippians.

But you should also know that we've been praying for you too. Really. We've been asking that the Lord will bring you to the same realization that led King David to say:

> *I know the LORD is always with me. I will not be shaken, for he is right beside me. No wonder my heart is filled with joy* (Psalm 16:8-9).

A Letter Between Friends

Whenever friends write letters, they leave a lot unsaid. Because the author and the recipient know each other, they can dispense with formalities and background information. They can make cryptic references to people, things, and events about which they share common knowledge. They can easily read between the lines because they both know the underlying context of what is being said.

Understanding doesn't come so easily, however, for a stranger who picks up a letter and tries to make sense of it. Reading such a letter usually produces more questions than information. It can be a frustrating experience. (Just ask any parent who has tried to decipher the letters found hidden in their teenager's sock drawer.)

You're about to read a great letter that was written by the apostle Paul to the members of the church at Philippi. Strangers, such as you, have been reading this letter for centuries and found encouragement and instruction from it. But you can glean much more from this little letter if you know what is going on between the lines.

You don't have to be a stranger any longer. In this chapter we'll give you the inside scoop. We'll give you the background so you can better understand what Paul is talking about. You'll have all of the information you need, and you won't have to go grubbing around in a sock drawer to find it.

Chapter 1

Philippians: Reading Between the Lines

What's Ahead

- Next Stop...Philippi

- Gone but Not Forgotten

- A Thank-You Letter and More

- What to Look For

The apostle Paul was not some slick self-help, talk-show guru with glib advice about finding true happiness. First of all, Paul wasn't peddling happiness. (As with most emotions, *happiness* can come and go depending upon your circumstances. Paul promoted *joy*—a confident stability that comes from knowing God is in control regardless of your circumstances.) Secondly, Paul wasn't some theoretical philosopher who pontificated from an ivory tower (or a television studio), far removed from the real world. As Paul wrote to the Philippians about joy in the midst of hardship, he was speaking from personal experience. His real-world scenario included being handcuffed to a soldier while he rotted away as a prisoner in Rome. But wait, we're getting ahead of ourselves.

The Author: A Roman, Jewish Christian

Except for Jesus, no person impacted the history of Christianity more than Paul. We'll talk more about his biography later, but here are a few facts that will help you in your overview of Philippians.

Paul was a Jew (from the tribe of Benjamin), and he was a devout Pharisee (the religious leaders of the Jews). Until his dramatic encounter with Christ, he was famous for persecuting Christians—with a vengeance. As a Christian missionary, he was responsible for bringing the Gospel message to Gentiles (refuting an erroneous view that salvation through Christ should be available only to Jews). Because his father was a Roman citizen, Paul inherited Roman citizenship. As you read Philippians, you'll see how Paul's Jewish and Roman backgrounds make his message particularly relevant to the Christians in Philippi.

Next Stop...Philippi

The year was A.D. 50—an exciting (but dangerous) time for the followers of Christ. In the 17 years or so since Christ's resurrection, the Gospel message had permeated the towns and villages in regions surrounding Jerusalem (despite opposition from the Jewish establishment). And thanks to missionaries like Paul and Silas, the story of the resurrection of Jesus Christ was beginning to spread like wildfire throughout the rest of the known world (to the chagrin of the Roman government).

Paul was on the second of his three missionary trips. Up to this point, he had restricted his travels to the cities of Eastern Asia. But while in the city of Troas (a seaport town on the eastern edge of Asia Minor), he received a vision from God to bring the Gospel to the region of Macedonia (now known as southeastern Europe in the area of northern Greece). Immediately Paul, accompanied by Silas, Luke, and Timothy, boarded a ship, and within two days they landed in the city of Philippi.

A Roman Colony

As the Roman Empire expanded, it established colonies in each new region. These were considered imperial cities within the regions (like a miniature Rome). Philippi had been a Roman colony in Macedonia since about 30 B.C. Most of the inhabitants were Roman citizens (brought in from Rome for official government business). They spoke their native language of Latin (rather than Greek), and they followed the fashions of Rome rather then wearing the apparel of the Macedonians. As a Roman colony, the Philippians enjoyed economic and political privileges that were not available to the other cities of the region. They could regulate their own affairs without much interference from the provincial governor. The Roman culture permeated this city to the core. Keep this in mind as you read Philippians (because Paul had it in mind as he wrote to the Christians in this city).

Starting a church from scratch is tough. Paul and his band of itinerant missionaries wandered into the town of Philippi as complete strangers. The city had no Christian church (or any Christians for that matter). They were about to make the very first formal presentation of the Gospel message in Europe, but they were going to have to do it in an informal manner—talking to people as they met them.

The story of the inception of the church at Philippi is told in Acts 16. You'll want to read that chapter to get some important background. There you'll discover some of the significant events that shaped the formation of the Philippian church and forged the close bond between Paul and its members:

- One of the first converts to Christianity in Philippi was a businesswoman by the name of Lydia. The fledgling church probably met in her home.

- The Philippian authorities unjustly arrested Paul and Silas. But their imprisonment resulted in the jailer (and his family) becoming Christians. Don't miss reading Acts 16:33-34, which tells how the jailer brought Paul and Silas into his home to wash their wounds and feed them a meal.

Lydia, the jailer, and their families were some of the first members of the church in Philippi (which was the first Christian church in Europe). With the hospitality of members like Lydia, and the compassion of members like the jailer, we should not be surprised that the Philippian Christians were renowned for their generosity and kindness.

Gone but Not Forgotten

Paul was in Philippi on that first visit for only about three months. But he forged friendships with the believers there that continued for the rest of his life. For these new Christians, Paul was like a spiritual older brother to them. They were ever grateful to him, and he considered them to be supporters of his missionary efforts in other regions.

That first visit by Paul was only the beginning of a lasting relationship between him and his friends in Philippi:

- After he left Philippi, Paul traveled to Thessalonica, where he spent several months. While there, he received several gifts from the Philippians to aid in his financial support.

- Later, while in Athens and in Corinth, he received more financial support from the Philippian Christians. Although Paul was often in need of support, sometimes the Philippians were the only church that helped him in a financial way.

- Paul made a second visit to Philippi when he was setting out on this third missionary journey.

- His third visit to the church in Philippi occurred when he was on his return trip on the third missionary journey.

- Although the historical record is sketchy, he might have made a fourth visit to the city. This was what he said he intended to do when he wrote to them (Philippians 2:19,24).

Paul has a fondness in his heart for his friends in Philippi. Like a parent who doesn't want to divulge that one of the kids is a favorite, Paul never admitted that he loved the Philippians more than the other churches that he visited. But you don't have to be a Bible scholar to know that this is how he felt. His true feelings are revealed in statements such as...

*Dear brothers and sisters, I love you and long to
see you, for you are my joy and the reward for
my work* (Philippians 4:1).

A Thank-You Letter and More

Paul's letter to the Philippians was written ten years
or so after his first visit to the city. At the time of writing
the letter, he was imprisoned in Rome. He had been in
prison for about two months or more. During that time,
the church in Philippi had sent him a financial gift via a
church member named Epaphroditus. And Epaphroditus
was himself part of the gift. In addition to being a messenger, he stayed and assisted Paul in the prison.

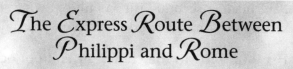

The Express Route Between Philippi and Rome

The distance between Philippi and Rome was about the same
as the distance between New York and Chicago (about 800
miles). Epaphroditus probably took about one month to make
the trip.

Paul had several reasons for writing a letter to the
Philippians from his jail cell. The specific purposes will
become obvious as you read the passages, but for now we
want you to get the overall picture:

- Being a Christian in the Roman Empire was not
  easy. Yet the Philippians were always making personal sacrifices to support Paul emotionally and
  financially. The gift brought by Epaphroditus was
  very meaningful to Paul, and he was compelled to
  convey his appreciation in writing.

- Epaphroditus gave Paul more than some cash. Without a doubt, he gave Paul a detailed report on the people and circumstances of the Philippian church. Most of it was good, but some of the relationships had a few rough spots. Paul used his letter as an opportunity to encourage the repair of some relationships in the church.

- When the church sent Epaphroditus to be an attendant for Paul, they expected Epaphroditus to stay with Paul for quite a while. But Epaphroditus became ill and almost died. News of this situation reached Philippi, and Paul knew that the church would be worried about Epaphroditus. And Epaphroditus was homesick and anxious to be back with his church family. One of the reasons underlying the letter (which Epaphroditus carried back with him to Philippi) was to ensure that the church knew that Epaphroditus had served Paul well even though his time with Paul was shorter than had been anticipated.

- Just as Paul was interested in what was happening in Philippi, the Philippians were curious about Paul's situation. How was he holding up in prison? What was his state of mind? What were his needs? How could they help? Of course, Epaphroditus would bring back a report, but they would appreciate reading Paul's own words.

- Remember that the church in Philippi was full of brand-new Christians. Although Luke and Timothy spent some extra time there, the Philippians didn't have a resident apostle (like the church in Jerusalem had with Peter). Wanting to reinforce proper doctrines and to protect the Philippians from false teachings, Paul devoted part of his letter to reinforcing some of the spiritual principles that the Philippians already knew.

What to Look For

Although Paul originally wrote Philippians to his friends in the church at Philippi, he knew that the letter would be circulated and read by other Christians in other churches. (Churches had a custom of sharing letters such as this so that everyone could benefit from the apostles' teachings.) Paul might have suspected a larger reading audience than just the Philippians, but he never imagined that you would be part of the audience. But God knew. So, as the Holy Spirit inspired Paul as he wrote the letter to the Philippians, you were part of the intended audience. With that in mind, you should read Philippians on two levels. First, read for what Paul wanted to communicate to his dear friends. But more important, read for what God wants you to learn.

On that second, deeper level, you have the opportunity to learn one of the greatest secrets of life. It was a secret that Paul learned from Christ, and Paul reveals that secret in the pages of Philippians. It is a secret that allowed Paul to say:

> *I have learned how to get along happily whether I have much or little...I have learned the secret of living in every situation...For I can do everything with the help of Christ who gives me the strength I need* (Philippians 4:11-13).

That's a secret worth knowing. Look for it as you read through Philippians.

■ ■ ■

Study the Word

1. Read Acts 16:6-40 for background on Paul's initial experiences in Philippi. In what ways did the encounter with Lydia and the jailer accelerate the formation of the Christian church in Philippi?

2. Philippi had a prohibition against bringing unrecognized religions into the city. How do you suppose Paul would have responded to a charge that Christianity was not a legitimate religion?

3. See Acts 16:13-15. Paul's first convert to Christianity in Europe appears to be a businesswoman named Lydia, and she apparently played a key role in the church. What does this tell you about God's view of women? What about Paul's view of women?

4. Refer to Acts 16:35-37. What was the strategy behind Paul refusing to leave the jail when he was allowed to do so?

5. Do a quick speed-read through Philippians. Make note of Paul's references to *joy* or *rejoicing*. Can you find 16 such references? Use these verses to compose a thesis statement for Philippians.

A Friendly Format

Writing letters back in the first century A.D. was a little different than now. Today, you'd probably dispense with a pen and paper and just use e-mail. Back then you'd use parchment and a crude writing implement, often making a mess when dipping the "pen" into a container of ink.

But the tools of writing aren't the only difference. The formats are also very dissimilar. Today we might use an abrupt "Hi" or "Dear So-and-So" before getting right to the point. But in Paul's time, letters customarily began with a lengthy salutation that described both the author and the audience. It also set the context and tone for the content that would follow.

In the first 11 verses of chapter 1 of Philippians, Paul says quite a lot. We are sure that the members of the church in Philippi found Paul's words to be both instructional and spiritually encouraging. We think you'll find them that way too. They certainly beat a spam e-mail about refinancing your mortgage.

Chapter 2

The Joy of Christian Partnership

Philippians 1:1-11

*W*hat's *A*head

- ☐ A Heartfelt Salutation (1:1-2)

- ☐ Thinking of You (1:3-8)

- ☐ Praying for You (1:9-11)

*A*pproximately one-third of the New Testament is comprised of letters that Paul wrote to individuals or churches. In any other situation, you might get in trouble if you were caught reading someone else's mail, but not when you are reading the letters *(epistles)* contained in the Bible. Paul wrote his letters knowing that they would be read by many people—that is how the teachings of Christianity spread so quickly and effectively in a society that lacked any means of mass communication. But that doesn't mean that his letters were generic. As you'll see from the first 11 verses of Philippians, Paul considered the Philippian Christians to be his partners in ministry, and he was not shy about saying how much he appreciated them.

A Heartfelt Salutation (1:1-2)

The "very truly yours" of Philippians is not at the end; it is in the very first verse. (In the first century A.D., letter writers often began by identifying themselves.) Paul says that the letter is from both "Paul and Timothy," but that doesn't mean that Timothy had any authorship. From verse 3 on, Paul uses the personal pronoun *I* and never *we*. Perhaps he makes reference to Timothy because...

- Timothy was living in Rome and providing care and companionship to Paul while he was in prison.

- Timothy was with Paul on that first visit to Philippi, so many of the Philippian church members personally knew Timothy and would be encouraged to know that he was with Paul.

- Timothy might have been the person who actually transcribed the letter as Paul dictated it. Many scholars believe that Paul had poor eyesight and used someone else to write down the words as he spoke them.

When many people identify themselves, they make some reference to their occupation (such as "Hi, I'm Pastor Mark Zoradi" or "I'm Professor Roger Post"). Paul could have referred to himself as an apostle (a rather prestigious distinction in the early Christian church). Instead, he identified himself as the *slave* of Jesus Christ (some Bible translations use the word *servant*). That puts Paul on the same level as Timothy and the people at Philippi. He was an apostle; they weren't. But they were all believers in Jesus Christ. Because this passage emphasizes how the Philippians were partners with Paul in his ministry, Paul wasn't going to pull rank on them. And being the servant of Jesus Christ is no cause for embarrassment. Serving the Savior is the highest of all privileges.

$\mathcal{A}$ Slave of Christ?

Paul uses the Greek word *doulos* to describe his relationship with Christ (1:1). Some scholars interpret *doulos* to mean "servant," but you'll get a better flavor for the word if you use the preferred translation of "slave." But don't picture a slave in the context of a vicious master who brutalizes his slave. In the spiritual context, a slave of Christ is one who ministers to the Lord voluntarily and out of appreciation.

You might think that *volunteer* would be a word that fits a Christian's relationship to Christ better than *slave*. Well, here is what Paul probably had in mind when he used the terminology:

- Christ paid a price for us (His blood on the cross).

- As Christians, we turn possession of our lives over to Him.

- By acknowledging Christ as our Savior, we owe absolute obedience to Him.

Paul never considered our slavery to Christ to be oppressive. Just the opposite. Only by giving our allegiance to Christ do we break free from the bondage of sin (Romans 6:5-11). To be the slave of Christ is to realize spiritual freedom.

Paul isn't writing to the community at large in Philippi. He is writing to the Christians there. Unlike our society, where Christians in a city might belong to different churches, Philippi had only one Christian church. Paul had founded this church, but it didn't fall apart in his absence. It had leaders who assumed responsibility for teaching and oversight. Paul includes a reference to these church leaders in his salutation (1:1), but Paul was writing to the entire church, not just the leaders.

Don't skip over the blessing Paul pronounced in verse 2. This was not merely a meaningless ritual (like saying "God bless you" after someone sneezes). Paul knew that his readers would understand the full meaning of...

> *Grace*: God's unmerited favor that is willingly and freely bestowed on us by His loving-kindness

> *Peace*: the sense of reconciliation with God and true spiritual wholeness that is available only through Christ's sacrifice on the cross

Thinking of You (1:3-8)

As famous as he was, Paul was no egotist. He knew that he owed everything to God, and he acknowledged his appreciation to God for the role the Philippians played in his ministry. Paul emphasizes his "partnership" relationship with the Philippians in this passage.

Partners in Spreading the Good News (1:3-5)

Paul was a missionary, commissioned by God to bring the Gospel message to Europe. As the first church in that region, the Philippians certainly assisted Paul in that task in the city of Philippi. They grew in their faith, and they were mature Christians. They did not damage the reputation of Christianity with immature behavior or polluted doctrine (as some other churches were doing). Thus, within their community of Philippi, these Christians were effective ambassadors of the Gospel and supported Paul's efforts.

But the partnership between Paul and the Philippian Christians extended beyond the borders of Philippi. Because they sent financial support to Paul while he was engaged in missionary efforts elsewhere, they were promoting his ministry throughout Europe and Asia Minor. They were truly his partners in *spreading* the Gospel message because they didn't selfishly restrict their efforts to their own city. They recognized Paul's effectiveness as an evangelist—he could get the message of Christ to regions they could never reach—and they enthusiastically supported him in those efforts.

Partners in God's Blessings (1:6-7)

At the moment they believe in Christ and turn control of their lives over to Him, Christians receive God's gift of salvation. Salvation happens completely and instantaneously. But another of God's gifts is *sanctification,* which is the process of becoming holy. Sanctification doesn't happen all at once; it involves the progressive development of learning how to live in a way that is pleasing and honoring to God. Paul knew that he was in this process (3:12), and his partners in Philippi were also "works in progress" under the craftsmanship of Christ.

Perhaps you've heard some Christians say, "God isn't finished with me yet." That's a true statement, but it shouldn't be used as an excuse. Instead, that statement represents the principle of sanctification. At no point while on this earth will we become all that Christ wants us to be, but we can be moving in that direction. That was the direction Paul and the Philippians were headed. That was what they shared in common, and that was why Paul was so confident in them.

Notice that Paul and the Philippians shared these blessings without regard to their personal circumstances. As Paul stated in 1:7, this happened whether he was in prison or out in the mission field. The blessings of God aren't affected by our situation, so we shouldn't lose our appreciation of those blessings when we encounter difficult circumstances.

Partners in Christ (1:8)

Most friendships are self-centered; people usually invest in a friendship only to the extent that they benefit from it. Seldom will an individual have a selfless devotion for someone else. But that happens when people are partners in Christ. Paul's affection for his friends in Philippi was so great that he compared it to the love of Christ.

We're sure that God was not offended when Paul wrote that he loved the Philippians as Christ loved them. That's exactly the type of relationship that God has in mind for believers. Christians' love for each other should cause the other people of the world to take notice. Christ is the common bond that makes Christians part of the same family. Love should be the primary and prominent characteristic of that family. Paul's affection for the Philippians was a fulfillment of Christ's instruction to His followers:

> *I have loved you even as the Father has loved me. Remain in my love. When you obey me, you remain in my love, just as I obey my Father and remain in his love. I have told you this so that you will be filled with my joy. Yes, your joy will overflow! I command you to love each other in the same way that I love you* (John 15:9-12).

Praying for You (1:9-11)

Moving from thoughts about the love that Christians share for each other, Paul concludes the opening passage of his letter by telling the Philippians how he prays for them. This is another way in which Paul displays his intense love for them. His strongest desire is that they mature in their relationship with God. A quick and easy paraphrase would be, "Love God more." But many people confuse love with an emotion. Paul gets more specific as he describes what loving God means practically. Toward that end, Paul prays that they will...

Grow in their knowledge of God. This kind of knowledge refers to gaining spiritual wisdom from studying Scripture (just like you're doing now).

Grow in their understanding of God. Here Paul is referring to spiritual insight—the practical application of spiritual wisdom. In other words, letting Scripture and the Holy Spirit help you apply spiritual principles to everyday life.

Discern what is pure and blameless. Paul isn't referring to perfectionism, and he doesn't expect that they will be sinless. Neither does God. Remember that sanctification is a process. Paul has their motives in mind, not their behavior.

Honor God by the way they live. Christianity is not about rules and regulations. It is about thinking correctly. When we reflect on what God has done for us through Christ's sacrifice on the cross, we should direct our motivation and thoughts toward honoring Christ. Right thinking—which produces right living—honors God.

Paul is building a set of bookends into this little letter. Here in chapter 1, he tells the Philippians that he is praying that they will understand what is best and really matters in life (1:10). He prays that they will be filled with the characteristics of Jesus Christ (1:11). We don't want to spoil the surprise for you, but that is exactly how he ends his letter. In chapter 4, he concludes with similar sentiments. He wants the Philippians to be thinking correctly so their lives honor God. And just so you don't stay in suspense, we'll give you a taste of what Paul means when he refers to the characteristics that he is praying will be evident in the lives of the Philippians (and you):

> *Fix your thoughts on what is true and honorable and right. Think about things that are pure and lovely and admirable. Think about things that are excellent and worthy of praise. Keep putting into practice all you learned from me and heard from me and saw me doing, and the God of peace will be with you* (Philippians 4:8-9).

▣ ▣ ▣

Study the Word

1. Paul begins Philippians differently than he begins most of his other letters. Read 1 Corinthians 1:1; 2 Corinthians 1:1; Galatians 1:1; Ephesians 1:1 and Colossians 1:1. What's the difference between these verses and Philippians 1:1? What do you think Paul had in mind when he intentionally made Philippians 1:1 different from his other salutations?

2. Do you sense that you are a partner in ministry with any other Christian? Describe the "who" and the "what" of this partnership.

3. Describe the ways in which you are growing as a Christian.

4. List a few characteristics of Christ that are evident in your life. List a few characteristics of Christ that you would like to see grow in your life.

5. Describe what being the servant or slave of Jesus Christ means.

ℒiving with ℒemons

We're fed up with the expression "If life gives you lemons, then make lemonade." First of all, we don't like lemonade. Secondly, often our "lemons" (the circumstances of our lives) are so dried up and rotten that we can't get a drop of juice regardless of how hard we squeeze.

Do you ever feel like that? Sometimes the situations of your life can be so tough that you can't imagine how anything good can come of them. If you find yourself in that spot, then the "turn lemons into lemonade" tidbit might tempt you into squeezing the neck of the person who says it.

In this next passage, Paul refers to his own personal circumstances. Life for him at the time he wrote Philippians was not easy. And life itself wasn't certain because he didn't know if an execution was in his future. But despite the situation, Paul could rejoice about it all. You'll enjoy reading his perspective. (And don't worry. He says it all without mentioning lemonade.)

The Joy of Difficult Circumstances

Philippians 1:12-30

- God Turns Bad Circumstances into Good Results (1:12-14)

- The Important Thing Is the Message (1:15-19)

- Life or Death—Either One Is Good (1:20-26)

- So No Matter What, Live like This (1:27-30)

*P*aul has shared his love and prayers with the Philippians, and now he responds to questions that he knows are on their minds. They know he is in prison in Rome. What they don't know is how he is holding up under those conditions. They've sent Epaphroditus with money and encouragement, but they're wondering if they can do something else. When will Paul's case come to trial? What will be the outcome? Does he expect the death penalty, an extended jail sentence, or a "not guilty" verdict? Will he ever be able to come back and see them? How can they be praying for him? And on a more theological level, why would God allow this to happen?

Paul doesn't have answers to their specific questions. But that doesn't matter because he has a perspective that makes their questions irrelevant.

God Turns Bad Circumstances into Good Results (1:12-14)

Imprisonment didn't bring a halt to Paul's missionary efforts; it just redirected the focus of his evangelistic efforts (and severely restricted his travel schedule). Because he was a Roman citizen, Paul had a little more freedom than most inmates. He was given the privilege of being under house arrest, which allowed him to live in a rented house. In his own home, Paul could have friends visit, and he wrote letters to his friends and churches. (His "prison epistles" include Colossians, Philemon, Ephesians, and Philippians.)

But Paul's house arrest had another, more subtle, benefit. Because the Jews characterized Paul as a dangerous troublemaker and dissident, the Roman officials chained him to a member of the praetorian guard (the elite Roman palace guard) 24 hours a day. Think of it. Three times a day the shift changed; a new soldier would be handcuffed to Paul for eight hours. During that time the soldier heard Paul speak with Timothy (and other visitors like Epaphroditus) about Christ. The soldiers heard Paul dictating his epistles. Paul had a captive audience—literally. Before long, members of the praetorian guard were accepting Christ. This wasn't just the case with one or two soldiers. Christianity swept through the entire palace guard. With this perspective, you can see why Paul didn't mind his handcuffs.

Why Was Paul in Prison?

Several years earlier, Paul had been arrested in Jerusalem. The Jewish leaders were enraged by Paul's claim that God's love was extended to the Gentiles. They had him arrested for inciting a riot (which they caused). As a Roman citizen, Paul was able to demand a trial before a Roman magistrate. Because he was a controversial figure in Palestine, Paul appealed his case to Caesar. He was dispatched to Rome with a military escort and delivered to the praetorian guard, where he was under house arrest while he awaited his trial. The story of the arrest in Jerusalem is reported in Acts 21:17–22:29. The house arrest in Rome is described in Acts 28:11-16.

The Important Thing Is the Message (1:15-19)

Bringing the Gospel message to the elite members of the Roman army was not the only benefit of Paul's imprisonment. His situation was encouraging other Christians to preach more boldly. Some did so with good motives; others had intentions that were less than honorable.

- Some people renewed their witnessing efforts out of their love and respect for Paul. They didn't want the spread of the Christian message to be deterred by Paul's incarceration, so they stepped to the line to take his place. Also, they knew that increasing their evangelistic efforts would be a spiritual encouragement to Paul.

- The motivations of some other Christians weren't so admirable. They intensified their preaching efforts because they sensed an opportunity to steal the spotlight from Paul. Apparently they had been jealous of the attention and success that followed

Paul's ministry. With him out of the picture, these other preachers could vie for top billing on the missionary circuit.

Paul doesn't let petty feelings overshadow the ultimate result. Regardless of the motives, He is pleased that his situation was the impetus for the message of Christ to be preached.

Notice that Paul's perspective finds the upside of his circumstances in the benefit to the cause of Christ. He isn't trying to find present good for *himself* in his tough times. Instead, he sees the present benefit for God's kingdom. From a personal standpoint, he can be confident about his future (even though he doesn't have a clue how it will turn out) because he is supported by the prayers of the Philippians and because he experiences the presence of the Holy Spirit.

Life or Death—Either One Is Good (1:20-26)

This passage hits one of the major themes of Philippians. The meaning of your existence doesn't get any more basic than life versus death. Some people want to live because they are afraid of death. Other people, contemplating suicide, want to die because they are afraid of life. Paul couldn't make up his mind between the two options, but not because he was afraid. He was torn because he saw benefits in both.

Paul's preference might have been for death because he was so anxious to be with Christ. For non-Christians, death usually implies the cessation of life: the end of the road, the grand finale, or as Porky Pig used to say... "That's all, folks." But for Christians, life is eternal. It starts at the moment of salvation and never stops (Romans 6:22-23). For Paul, physical death was a nonevent. Whenever it happened, his spiritual life would continue and he would have his desired bonus of being in the presence of Christ.

But Paul knew that the Philippians would benefit if he continued living. As long as he was alive, he would be preaching and teaching about Christ. He loved the Philippians so much that he was willing to live—if that was what God wanted—so he could help them grow and mature in their faith. Paul had found the secret to a joyful life, and he was willing to postpone being in heaven for the sake of the Philippians so he could help them experience joy in the same way (1:25).

Notice that Paul's quandary between life and death has nothing to do with his tangible circumstances. For him, the logistics of life are irrelevant. His imprisonment situation doesn't even enter into the analysis of whether he would rather "live for Christ" or "die to be with Christ." He does not say, "Living would be better if I could be freed from house arrest." Neither does he say, "Well, if I've got to stay in chains for the rest of my life, then I'd prefer death." Instead, Paul evaluates everything from an eternal perspective.

If Paul were writing to you today, his jargon might change a bit. He might say something like, "It's not about me. It's all about Christ." And that seems to be the message that Paul wants us to take away from this passage. Our circumstances should not dictate our moods or our emotions or our outlook. We shouldn't see them as insurmountable obstacles. In fact, we should hardly notice them at all. Our perspective should be so Christ-focused that any present difficulties or unfortunate circumstances become blurred in our peripheral vision. We should find our joy and confidence in Christ. Then we can relate to Paul when he says, *"My life will always honor Christ, whether I live or I die"* (1:20).

Is God Responsible for Every Bad Circumstance?

Absolutely not! God is sovereign, so nothing happens in our lives that He doesn't allow. But many times He doesn't initiate the problems that we're going through. Sometimes, tough situations are the result of Satan trying to make our lives difficult to see if we'll turn away from God in the process. (If you think we're kidding, then read about the life of Job in the Old Testament.) Other times, not even Satan is to blame; some of our problems are just the result of our own dumb choices. But whether tough times are brought about by God, by Satan, or by ourselves, we can bring honor to God by the way we respond.

So No Matter What, Live like This (1:27-30)

Reading the end of the previous passage (1:25-26) might give the impression that Paul was confident that he would be returning to Philippi. He obviously wanted that result for their benefit, but he couldn't speak with such assurance when his future was so uncertain. So, at this point, he wants to prepare them for the possibility that he might not return to Philippi...ever.

Paul begins this "regardless of what happens to me" passage by encouraging the Philippians to conduct themselves like ambassadors of Christ. His puts this charge in the context of citizenship. The Philippians certainly knew about citizenship. They were Roman citizens who lived in a Roman colony. They lived far from Rome, but everything about them reflected pride in their Roman citizenship: their language (Latin), their fashion, their names, and their customs. Paul artfully analogizes their Christianity to the importance of their Roman citizenship. He says that they should at all times behave like citizens of heaven.

Paul then gives them some specific examples of what Christian citizenship is all about:

- They are to stand firm in their faith. Even if the going gets tough, they should not abandon their beliefs. They are to be proactive in influencing their culture.

- They should stand together in unity. Christianity is a team sport. It was not intended to be played alone. No one knew this point better than Paul. That is why he was so appreciative of their support of his ministry.

- They are to be confident in their faith. He does not want them to be intimidated by their enemies.

Although Paul was able to overlook the difficulties of his life situation, he knew that the Philippians might not yet be mature enough to see past tough circumstances. So, he doesn't minimize the fact that life is hard for them. He doesn't downplay their problems. He simply reminds them that to suffer for Christ is a privilege. Then, to illustrate the points he has just made about Christian citizenship, he emphasizes that he is fighting with them in the struggle.

Paul's message to the Philippians is equally relevant to you. God knows if you are going through struggles and tough times. He doesn't expect you to ignore them. You shouldn't pretend that they don't exist. But you shouldn't let these obstacles impede your spiritual growth. To the contrary, you should stand firm and confident. Realize that the privilege of knowing Christ affords you the privilege of trusting Him through your problems. Use these difficulties as an opportunity to be dependent on Christ and interdependent with other Christians. Then you will begin to experience a sense of joy—not from knowing how things will turn out but from an eternal perspective that puts your focus on Christ.

■ ■ ■

Study the Word

1. Are you in the middle of tough circumstances? What adversities are confronting you? In what way is your Christian faith a help in these problems?

2. Paul was comforted in his tough circumstances by the presence of the Holy Sprit. Read John 16:5-15, in which Jesus tells the disciples that He is sending the Holy Spirit to be their Comforter in His absence. What is Jesus trying to tell the disciples? What is the connection between what Jesus explained and what Paul felt?

3. What is your perspective about death? Are you afraid of it or looking forward to it? If Paul knew what you were thinking about life and death, what do you think he would say to you?

4. Do you think experiencing joy in the middle of adversity is really possible? Why or why not?

5. What are some practical ways in which you can maintain a Christ-focused perspective during tough times?

Team Players

Teamwork. It is an essential ingredient of any human organization. Whether the group is a sports team, a business, or a church, it won't function well if every person is pursuing selfish goals. A united purpose is essential. All members must be working in unity toward a common goal.

In chapter 2 of Philippians, Paul has unity on his mind. You'll read how he suggests that humility is the best foundation for unity. And perhaps just to be on the safe side, so no member of the Philippian church could brag about being the most humble, Paul uses Jesus Christ as the ultimate example of humility.

It would be easy to read Philippians 2 as Paul's admonitions to the members of the church at Philippi. But don't take such a restricted view. Study this chapter as if Paul is speaking directly to you. You'll be spiritually encouraged by the insights of Christ's humility, and your church may be better off as you learn principles about building unity with your fellow Christians.

One word of caution: Be careful as you read this chapter. Humility is a tricky thing. The instant you take pride in the fact that you have acquired it, you've automatically lost it.

Chapter 4

The Joy of Unity

Philippians 2

*P*aul did not love the Philippians because they were a perfect church. Oh, maybe they had fewer problems than other churches, but they still needed Paul's coaching on some doctrinal issues and some relational matters. We'll get to the theological topic in the next chapter, but this point in Paul's letter allowed him to gracefully segue to the subject of interpersonal relationships.

Humility Is the Foundation for Unity (2:1-4)

The clues seem to indicate that disunity threatened the Philippian church. Apparently the members were arguing (see 2:14 and 4:2). To address this problem, Paul moves deftly from talking about their partnership with him in ministry (1:3-11) and their shared struggles (1:30), to the importance of unity. In Paul's view, you can't have joy ministering for Christ if you're at odds with the people who are ministering with you. Just as you can find joy in your relationship with Christ, you can also find it in your relationship with your Christian brothers and sisters.

Paul begins by identifying the basis for our unity in Christ (2:1). As Christians, we have so much in common:

- We all belong to the same spiritual family.

- We are all loved by Christ.

- We have the unifying element of the Holy Spirit.

- We should be exhibiting the Christlike traits of love and compassion.

He concludes (in 2:2) that these commonalities should result in:

- wholehearted agreement among Christians

- love for one another

- a common heart, purpose, and passion for ministering together

Knowing that the Philippians would be anxious to please him, Paul declares that seeing these traits in their church would bring him true joy.

By the way, this wasn't a brand-new thought. Christ taught that the love and commitment of Christians for each other should be something that the rest of the world notices. Listen to what He said to the disciples on the night before He was crucified:

> *Love each other. Just as I have loved you, you should love each other. Your love for one another will prove to the world that you are my disciples* (John 13:34-35).

Knowing that unity doesn't come naturally—or easily—Paul gives a few more guidelines:

- Don't be selfish.

- Don't be hypocritical (trying to make yourself look better than you are).

- Be more interested in others than in yourself.

Notice the parallelism with the previous passage (1:12-30). Paul had just finished saying that to find joy in the midst of adversity, you have to forget about yourself and focus on Christ. Now he is saying that if you want to find joy in ministry, you have to forget about yourself and focus on the people you are ministering with.

The point Paul is making can be summed up in one word: *humility*. While pride distorts our view of ourselves and others, humility is a mind-set that keeps our relationship with God and with others in the proper perspective.

Christ Is the Epitome of Humility (2:5-11)

No example of humility tops that of Jesus Christ. Paul knew it, and so did the Philippians, but Paul couldn't resist the opportunity to raise Christ as the ultimate example.

The passage of Philippians 2:5-11 is instructive on several levels. Certainly it illustrates Christ's supreme display of humility by relinquishing His position in heaven for the ultimate suffering of death on the cross. But the passage also gives us important information about what happened when Christ became man. Paul mentions these factors:

- Christ was with God from the beginning.

- Christ and God are equal.

- Although He was God, Christ voluntarily came to earth in human form as part of God's plan for the salvation of humanity.

- By coming to earth, Christ voluntarily divested Himself of many of His Godly attributes.

- Christ did not merely assume a human costume. He really became a man.

- Christ died a physical and actual death by crucifixion. God accepted the blood of this innocent Man as the penalty for our sins. Christ died so that we wouldn't have to face eternal death.

- God has restored Christ to His rightful place in heaven, and at some time in the future the entire universe will acknowledge Christ's Lordship.

Try Putting That to Music

Some scholars believe that the words of Philippians 2:6-11 were verses from a hymn sung by Christians in the first century A.D. If that theory is correct, then Paul's use of those verses would have reminded the Philippians of certain truths that they were very familiar with.

Imagine if you were asked, for the sake of science, to undergo an experiment that would transform you into a garden slug. You would probably recoil at the mere suggestion of the indignity of it all. And why shouldn't you? You are a human being—the most advanced creature living on earth. Nothing could motivate you to undergo something so drastic and demeaning. Well, morphing you into a slug doesn't even approach the extent of the humiliation that Christ endured in coming to earth as a human and dying on the cross. We are completely unable to comprehend it. But to the extent that we can understand Christ's attitude, we are to emulate it.

You shouldn't gloss over two bonus features of this passage:

- Philippians 2:7 explains that Christ "emptied himself" of some of His divine characteristics. This is a theological point that has had Bible scholars scratching their heads and stroking their beards for centuries. While on earth, Jesus was all God and all man at the same time. His divine nature was revealed by His sinlessness. His human nature was revealed by physical characteristics such as hunger, thirst, and pain. He didn't use His divine nature to make His human life any easier. He chose not to use some of His divine characteristics, such as omnipotence (being all powerful) and omniscience (being all knowing).

- If you want to know how the world is going to end, take a peek at Philippians 2:9-11. Those verses describe the culmination of what the entire universe and God's plan are all about.

A Call to Unity (2:12-18)

Having presented Christ as the model for humility, Paul now challenges his dear friends in Philippi to make every effort to achieve unity in their church. Paul doesn't mean that they have to work to obtain their salvation. That already happened when they accepted Christ as their Savior. There is no To Do list that is required for salvation. This is clear from statements made by Paul to other churches:

> *God saved you by his special favor when you believed. And you can't take credit for this; it is a gift from God. Salvation is not a reward for the good things we have done, so none of us can boast about it* (Ephesians 2:8-9).

When Paul challenges them to work at their salvation (2:12), he is talking about the effort that is necessary to become more Christlike. He is referring to the sanctification process of progressive spiritual development that he spoke of earlier (see 1:6).

The people of the world are engaged in arguments and conflicts. Christians shouldn't be like that. Paul wants these Philippians to conduct themselves in such a way that they are positive influences in the pagan culture.

Knowing that the Philippians wouldn't want to disappoint him, Paul says that their behavior will determine if his ministry has ultimate meaning. If his life were a race, he would consider himself a loser at the finish line if they hadn't followed Christ's pattern. Obviously, God wouldn't judge Paul harshly if the Philippians had gone off the deep end. He wouldn't be a loser in God's eyes. But the Philippians knew that they were special to Paul, and they knew he would be disappointed if they ignored his teaching and influence. They wouldn't want him to feel that his ministry was in vain.

Does Your Life Reflect Salvation?

Paul has given the Philippians—and you—a checklist for evidence that Christ is in control of your life. The list isn't exhaustive, but he mentions some of the characteristics that should be showing through in your life.

1. Christians should be making some effort to grow spiritually (2:12).

2. Christians should have an attitude of reverence and awe regarding matters of their spiritual maturity (2:12). This is not an attitude of fear of punishment, but a fear of allowing sin to interrupt an intimate relationship with God.

3. The life of a Christian should reflect peace and tranquility (2:14). We shouldn't be known for being contentious or complaining.

4. The conduct of a Christian should be pure and wholesome (2:15). This applies not only to our conduct but also to our thoughts and motives.

5. Christians should be interested in being witnesses for Christ to nonbelievers (2:15). In other words, we should have a missionary mentality. No overseas travel is required. Sharing the message of Christ with your family and friends is enough.

If this was an evaluation checklist for your life, what kind of grade would you get?

Paul had earlier referred to the possibility of death, and he does so again in this passage. (Caesar could have decreed Paul's execution at any time, so the subject naturally comes up often.) In this instance, Paul says that his death will have meaning if his efforts caused the Philippians to walk closely with God. Here again Paul speaks of rejoicing in death for the cause of Christ.

Examples of Humility in Action (2:19-28)

Paul concludes this passage by giving two real-life examples of Christians who are on the right path: Timothy and Epaphroditus. They exemplify everything that Paul has been talking about. If fact, each would score very well on that lifestyle evaluation checklist in the box on page 49.

Notice what you can learn about the character of Timothy. Paul describes him in a way that fits the profile of a humble Christian:

- He must have had a pleasant attitude or else Paul wouldn't have used him as an emissary.

- He was willing to be Paul's messenger boy. Although he was a capable spiritual leader, he was willing to take a subservient role in Paul's ministry.

- He had a love for other Christians. Paul said that no one loved the Philippians more than Timothy.

- He consistently showed Christlike qualities. His reputation was established in this regard.

Probably a leader in the Philippian church, Epaphroditus was well-known to the members of the church in Philippi. As with Timothy, the circumstances of Paul's relationship with Epaphroditus speak highly of his Christian character:

- Epaphroditus was a man of humility. He was willing to put his life in Philippi on hold in order to visit Paul. He was willing to serve in whatever way would be helpful.

- His church family was very important to him. While he might have preferred to stay with Paul, he was returning to Philippi because he knew his friends were worried about his health.

- Epaphroditus must have had a personality that reflected Christ. Paul knew that the Christians of Philippi would be anxious for Epaphroditus to return home. This wouldn't have been the case if he had been a whiner and a complainer.

■ ▨ ▧

Study the Word

1. Why is unity important in a church? Does unity require everyone to think the same way? How can differences of opinions be expressed while maintaining unity?

2. Give a definition for Christian humility. Why does Paul consider humility to be the foundation for unity?

3. Isaiah 53 is a prophecy about the suffering that the Messiah would endure. Read that passage and describe how it relates to the humility that Christ exhibited.

4. In what ways did Paul, Timothy, and Epaphroditus display humility?

5. Review the Christian character traits in the box on page 49. Which of the traits would you like to develop in your life? How will you go about making the changes you desire?

Keeping Score

Many people have a difficult time accepting God's grace. To be sure, they appreciate God's gift of salvation, but they want to earn it through some sort of effort on their part. Why? Well, maybe our efforts make us feel superior to those who haven't done the work. If God's salvation is a gift and available to everyone, then we don't have anything over anyone else. But if we have to do something for salvation, then we're ahead of those who haven't done it.

Paul warns the Philippians against this mentality. Basically, he says: "Don't get caught up in the false teaching that you have to do certain things for salvation. Joy comes from realizing that Christ has done it all."

What about you? Don't think that church attendance, Bible study (devotions), or putting money in the offering can earn your salvation. These are good things to do, but they don't count as points on a salvation scorecard. Christ has taken care of everything necessary for your salvation. All you have to do is put your faith in Him. After that you can relax—and rejoice—in the fact that He has done it all.

Keep this in mind as you read this chapter: *You can do nothing to make Christ love you more, and you can do nothing to make Christ love you less.*

Chapter 5

The Joy of Being in Christ

Philippians 3:1-11

*W*hat's *A*head

☐ Beware of False Teaching (3:1-3)

☐ Human Effort Means Nothing (3:4-8)

☐ Christ's Work Means Everything (3:9-11)

*H*aving addressed some of the personal relationship issues in Philippians 2, Paul is now ready to tackle some doctrinal problems. In the first 11 verses of chapter 3, he is going to dispel a theological error that would surely sap the joy out of the Philippians' lives if it wasn't corrected. (By the way, if your Christian life seems mundane and sometimes oppressive, this passage may contain what you need to bring excitement back to your faith.)

Beware of False Teaching (3:1-3)

Before he begins to correct some misguided thinking, Paul hammers again on his theme of joy. This is something that is so inherent in a properly lived Christian life that Paul does not want them to miss it. He makes no apology for repeating it. In fact, he says that this theme bears repeating because it is so essential.

Paul wanted his dear friends to experience the joy of the Christian life. For them to do so, he knew that they must be warned about the dangerous traps that could drag them into despair. He has already hit two major joy squelchers:

- difficult circumstances and adversities

- disputes and friction with other Christians

Now, he brings up a third threat to a Christian's joy: the misguided notion that you must do certain things to earn your salvation. In particular, first-century Christians debated whether male Gentiles had to follow the Jewish rite of circumcision in order to be saved.

A group known as the Judaizers promoted this fallacy. Theirs was a minority viewpoint, and a wrong one at that. At the first official council of Christian believers in Jerusalem, the apostles decided that Gentiles did not need to follow the laws of Moses as a prerequisite to salvation. (See Acts 15.) Nonetheless, the Judaizers clung to this false doctrine, perhaps because...

- They had been devout practicing Jews, and they refused to concede that God was more interested in their inward attitudes than their outward performance.

- They thought that grace made salvation too easy for the Gentiles. They didn't like the idea that the Gentiles could so easily come to God without going through rules and regulations that the Judaizers had abided by for so long.

- They were afraid that if too many Gentiles became Christians, the faith would lose its Jewish influence.

- As long as Jewish rituals were a precondition for salvation, the Judaizers would have clout, authority, and leverage over the Gentile Christians.

Where Did the Judaizers Come Up with This Idea?

The big issue underlying Philippians 3:1-11 is the false teaching of the Judaizers. After Paul started a church, trained leaders, and moved on to the next town, the Judaizers would infiltrate. They taught that Gentiles could be saved only after they had complied with certain Jewish rituals. In particular, they said that Gentile men could not be saved until they were circumcised. Their doctrine was completely opposite from what Paul taught, and they confused the young Christians.

- For centuries, the Jews had operated under the Old Testament, which required them to perform certain rituals (circumcision of newborn males, sacrifices at the temple, feasts and ceremonies, and the like).

- Then along came Jesus, who showed that the purpose of the Ten Commandments and the laws of the Old Testament was to prove that humanity couldn't live up to God's perfect standard of holiness. We could never be good enough for God.

- Consequently, Jesus died on the cross to pay the penalty for our sins. (The ceremonial animal sacrifices of the past were images of His ultimate sacrifice.)

- Jesus' followers acknowledged Him to be the Messiah that the Jews had been awaiting for hundreds of years.

- Those first Christians were Jews, and some of them wondered if non-Jews (Gentiles) could become Christians. But in a specific vision (Acts 10), God revealed to Peter that His salvation was available to everyone, Jew and Gentile alike.

From this background, the Judaizers argued that Gentiles could be eligible for salvation only through the Jewish rituals (sort of like going through the initiation ceremony to be a member in a college fraternity).

Human Effort Means Nothing (3:4-8)

Like a father who protects his children from evil influences, Paul disparages the Judaizers and dismantles their arguments. Beginning at 3:4, Paul sets out his biographical profile from his life prior to becoming a Christian. These are credentials that would have placed him in the *Who's Who of True-Blooded Jews*:

1. *He was circumcised when he was eight days old.* Paul probably mentioned circumcision first because it was a big deal for the Judaizers. Being circumcised at eight days old according to the laws of Moses proved that Paul was a Jew from the time of his birth. A convert to Judaism would have been circumcised at the time of his conversion.

2. *He was born into a pure-blooded Jewish family.* Both of his parents were Jews. This was probably not true for many of the Judaizers. Paul could trace his ancestry all the way back to Abraham (2 Corinthians 11:22).

3. *He was a descendant of the tribe of Benjamin.* Among Jews, this tribe had a special place of honor and esteem because it produced Israel's first king.

4. *He was a "Hebrew of Hebrews."* In the previous century or so, many of the Jews had adopted Greek customs and abandoned their native Hebrew language. Not Paul. Hebrew was his native tongue, and he thoroughly knew the customs of his people.

5. *He was a member of the Pharisees.* With regard to keeping the Jewish laws, this was the strictest sect among the Jews. They even added their own set of regulations in addition to the laws of Moses. Compared to the devout Pharisees, the Judaizers were rookie legalists.

6. *He was a zealous Jew.* He was not only a Jew by birth and a Pharisee but also a *militant* Jew. Before he encountered Christ, Paul was the most feared, voracious, and relentless persecutor of the Christians.

7. *He was faultless.* Paul doesn't mean that he was sinless. He is merely stating that he was righteous from a legalistic point of view—he followed the rules precisely. This is a claim that the Judaizers couldn't make for themselves.

From a Jewish point of view, these credentials are impeccable. But Paul says they are worthless; they are like filthy rags. In fact, anything and everything that a person can do is worthless in comparison to knowing Christ.

If My Efforts Are Meaningless, Why Bother with Them?

Don't misunderstand Paul. When he says that human efforts are like garbage, he isn't advocating a slothful lifestyle. He isn't suggesting that you just sit back on your spiritual heinie and leave all of the work of Christianity to God. (Hey, if you can't get credit for it, why do it?)

Absolutely not. Any notion along those lines runs contrary to Paul's life and his teaching. Paul is all about "working hard," "pressing on," "running the race," and "straining to reach the goal." (More about that in the next chapter.) So, what's the distinction? Simply this: As far as *salvation* is concerned, our efforts count for nothing.

The things we do as Christians (sometimes referred to as our *works*) don't earn our salvation, but they provide proof of our salvation. In other words, if you are wondering whether you are saved or not, then look at your life: Are you exhibiting the kind of conduct that should be seen in the life of a Christian? James 2:14-17 says that our works provide a sort of litmus test for our faith:

> Dear brothers and sisters, what's the use of saying you have faith if you don't prove it by your actions? That kind of faith can't save anyone. Suppose you see a brother or sister who needs food or clothing, and you say, "Well, good-bye and God bless you; stay warm and eat well"—but then you don't give that person any food or clothing. What good does that do? So you see, it isn't enough just to have faith. Faith that doesn't show itself by good deeds is no faith at all—it is dead and useless.

Our efforts (or lack of them) won't change God's love for us, but we should be anxious to do them because we love Him.

Christ's Work Means Everything (3:9-11)

Is Paul guilty of false modesty? After all, according to Jewish tradition, he was part of the religious elite. And from a Christian perspective, he was one of the faith's greatest missionaries. Certainly all of those accomplishments must count for something, right? Well, Paul says they don't, and he ought to know.

Paul's doctrine of salvation is summed up in Philippians 3:9:

> *I no longer count on my own goodness or my ability to obey God's law, but I trust Christ to save me.*

It is as simple as that. We can do nothing to earn our salvation. From God's spiritual perspective, our actions are graded on a pass-fail basis, and all of us fail. (Admit it. As good as you are, you probably fall far short of Paul's religious credentials. If he couldn't make the cut, none of us can.)

God has done everything that is necessary for our salvation: He put the plan in place, He accepted Christ's death as the penalty for our sin, He offers salvation to us freely, He declares us to be blameless and righteous when we accept Christ as our Savior, He forgives and forgets our sins, He gives us eternal life. The list goes on and on. You can't take credit for any part of your salvation. The only part you play is to accept God's offer of salvation (and you couldn't even do that without the conviction of the Holy Spirit).

Through the salvation that Christ offers freely to us, we have the tremendous opportunity of knowing Christ. Through Him we can experience God's supernatural power. Then we will discover how much we depend on Him, and all of our accomplishments will suddenly vanish in significance.

Paul was not counting on anything that he had ever done to win favor with God. He trusted on Christ alone for his salvation. That realization is what kept Paul rejoicing. (Speaking of joy...we're sure that the Judaizers lost theirs as soon as the Philippians read Paul's letter for the first time in their church. That sound you hear is the door slamming as the Judaizers sneak out the rear exit.)

What About You?

Don't think that this false teaching of the Judaizers is irrelevant for the twenty-first century. Oh, sure, nobody in the church proclaims today that circumcision and other Jewish rituals are prerequisites for salvation. But what about other (more contemporary) things?

We suffer from the "Judaizer mentality" when we feel like Christianity is all about things we have to do or things we cannot do. We risk losing the joy of our salvation when we make Christianity a burdensome religion of rules and regulations instead of a vibrant faith that comes freely from God. As a Christian, you'll want to change the way you think and behave as your love for Christ grows deeper. But in the meanwhile, don't let other people (or yourself) oppress your faith with rules that God never intended.

Study the Word

1. What is the predominant feeling that your faith produces in your life? Is it joy? Is it something else? If your Christianity isn't a cause for rejoicing, what do you think is the problem?

2. What are some of the rules and regulations that people try to attach to Christianity in the twenty-first century? Have you ever been a victim—or a promoter—of the "Judaizer mentality"?

3. Have you ever taken pride in any of your Christian accomplishments? What are the dangers of thinking that these efforts can contribute toward your salvation?

4. Why do people struggle to accept the fact that God offers salvation as a gift?

5. Read Acts 15:1-35 for the story of the Council at Jerusalem and its declaration that circumcision was not a prerequisite for salvation. What was the reasoning and basis for their declaration? (Bonus points: Why did they suggest that the new Gentile Christians abstain from eating food that had been offered to idols?)

$\mathcal{P}$aul, the $\mathcal{P}$ersonal $\mathcal{T}$rainer

You don't have to be athletic to enjoy a good sports analogy. Nothing in Scripture indicates that Paul actually participated in any athletic endeavors (except perhaps "mental sparring" with the Judaizers). But that didn't keep him from using sports (such as running or boxing) as metaphors for the Christian life.

The passage you are about to read contains one of Paul's more famous athletic references. You'll find it in Philippians 3:13-14. Read it. Memorize it. Depend upon it.

Chapter 6

The Joy of Walking
with Christ

Philippians 3:12-21

*P*aul has just finished explaining that our accomplishments are worthless when it comes to salvation (3:1-11). Salvation is all God's doing; our only
participation involves putting our faith in Christ. Now,
Paul is ready to move the discussion along to the next
logical step. Actually, he'll be referring to many steps:
the steps we take on life's spiritual journey that happens
between salvation and when we'll be joined with Christ
in heaven. We often refer to this as our "Christian walk,"
but Paul uses the metaphor of running a race.

Going for the Prize (3:12-14)

In Philippians 3:10, Paul expressed his desire to know Christ. Now he lets the Philippians know that the knowledge of Christ doesn't happen overnight. Certainly salvation happens in an instant, but a complete understanding of who Christ is can't be accomplished in a lifetime. Fortunately, Christians will have an eternity to get to know Him. In the meantime, while we are on earth, learning more about Christ is a continual process.

When Paul talks about knowing Christ, he's referring to more than a passing acquaintance. His terminology also implies being like Christ. Here, again, Paul is talking about something that takes a lifetime (and we'll still fall short of Christ's character). As we learn to allow the Holy Spirit to have greater control in our lives, we move in the right direction, but battling our old sinful nature is a constant struggle. Paul was always up-front about his struggles in this regard:

> *I don't understand myself at all, for I really want to do what is right, but I don't do it. Instead, I do the very thing I hate...When I want to do good, I don't. And when I try not to do wrong, I do it anyway...It seems to be a fact of life that when I want to do what is right, I inevitably do what is wrong...Who will free me from this life that is dominated by sin? Thank God! The answer is in Jesus Christ our Lord* (Romans 7:15-25).

Recognizing that he has much more to learn about Christ and that he falls far short of being like Christ, Paul acknowledges that he is not perfect and hasn't attained complete knowledge of Christ.

But he wants to (and he assumes the Philippians want to as well). So he presses on in his Christian walk. With all his energies and a single-minded focus, he pursues knowing Christ. He is like an athlete in training, and here is his workout regimen:

- *He forgets the past.* An athlete won't make much progress in training if he or she is always focused on the defeats of the past. Paul knew this. Before his conversion, he persecuted Christians and participated in their executions. He could have been preoccupied with guilt, but he wasn't going to let Satan distract him with past failures.

- *He looks forward to what lies ahead.* Here Paul conveys the picture of a runner who is straining with 100 percent effort to move ahead in the race. He is keeping his eye on the finish line. He won't be distracted from proceeding in the race (of knowing Christ).

- *His goal is the prize.* Paul isn't running the race half-heartedly. He is running to get the prize. What is the prize of the Christian life? It is not heaven (although that is a nice benefit). In Paul's analogy, the prize is knowing Christ and being like Him. That is a prize that we won't obtain until we're with Christ in heaven. And that is why Paul keeps running in the meantime.

Walking in Maturity (3:15-16)

Do these two verses seem to interrupt the flow a little bit? Many Bible scholars think that Paul was making a slight diversion with these verses to take a few jabs at people with a different viewpoint about knowing Christ.

Apparently some people were attempting to tell the Philippians that achieving spiritual perfection (complete Christlikeness) on earth was possible.

Paul takes two shots at his opponents. First, he says that they are being spiritually naive. Actually, he doesn't demean them directly. He just says that all mature Christians will agree with the points he has made. Paul was big on maturity. (After all, isn't that the point of the Christian walk?) He must have been frustrated by the immature Christians who didn't know Christ well enough to have their doctrine straight. His solution, both for his opponents and for the Christians who might be influenced by them, was to encourage more spiritual growth. Here is what Paul said when he wrote to the Christians in Corinth on a slightly different doctrinal issue:

> *Dear brothers and sisters, don't be childish in your understanding of these things. Be innocent as babies when it comes to evil, but be mature and wise in understanding matters of this kind* (1 Corinthians 14:20).

Paul gave a second hit to his opponents. He said that if anyone had a different opinion on these matters, then God would eventually bring them around to the correct way of thinking (Paul's view).

Paul concludes this little digression by encouraging these people to continue on in their spiritual journey. Practically speaking, Paul is telling them to "keep on walking with the Lord." In other words, Paul isn't worried about their intentions if they are truly following after Christ. He doesn't need to get into a shouting match with them over this theological point. He has complete confidence that God will correct their thinking as they grow in spiritual maturity.

Walking Carefully (3:17-19)

Having finished his diversion, Paul gets back on track. He resumes his "training manual" for encouraging the Philippians in their walk with Christ. At this point, he suggests that they look to him as a personal trainer and that they avoid others who would definitely divert them from the goal of knowing Christ better.

We have learned to be careful when someone holds himself up as an example. People who do this usually want to be on a pedestal, and they seek (and need) the adulation of others. Those are the people who shouldn't be role models. In this passage, Paul tells the Philippians to emulate the way that he walks with Christ. Paul isn't making this suggestion out of conceit. Just the opposite. He does so from a spirit of humility:

- Remember that he earlier wrote that all of his accomplishments were as significant as a pile of filthy rags.

- And he has just finished saying that he has not attained perfection in the matter of knowing Christ. He admits that he is a work in progress, and he readily acknowledges that he has a long way to go.

With those imperfections, you might think that he is disqualified as a role model. Not so, because he wants them to copy the intention and motivation of his walk. He wants them to pattern their training regimen after his, which includes forgetting the past, looking forward, straining to move ahead, and racing to win the prize of knowing Christ (Philippians 4:13-14).

This is a serious matter for Paul. We know so because he admits to weeping over his concern for the Philippians in this regard. Why does this issue make him so intensely emotional? Here's why: If the Philippians don't follow his example, they may end up following others who Paul considers to be "enemies of the cross of Christ." These would be people in the church who lived selfish lives without any restraint. Scholars believe that Paul was referring to *antinomians* who were against all laws. In Paul's mind, these people weren't walking with Christ; they were headed in the opposite direction.

Look at how Paul describes the antinomians. (By the way, this is a good checklist for us to use in evaluating whether we are following a Christlike role model).

- They are ruled by their appetites. This isn't a reference to their eating habits. It is a metaphor that goes beyond gluttony. Paul is saying that they cater to their carnal and sensual desires. They follow their natural desires and instincts for pleasure in any form.

- They revel in their unbridled and immoral practices. They joke about them. They brag about them. They have no shame or guilt about them.

- Their minds are on the here and now. They have no eternal perspective. Consequently, they focus on sensual pursuits instead of having an eternal, spiritual focus on knowing Christ.

Understandably, Paul is of the opinion that these people are headed for eternal destruction. And that is precisely why Paul wants the Philippians to follow his walk with Christ rather than their path to spiritual devastation.

Keeping in Mind Where the Walk Will End (3:20-21)

The antinomians probably made fun of Paul (behind his back) as being so heavenly minded that he couldn't have any earthly fun. Paul would undoubtedly counter that the antinomians were so earthly minded that they had no connection with heaven. Christians may live on earth, but they have citizenship in heaven from the moment of their salvation. Paul concludes this discourse on walking with Christ by reminding the Philippians of their ultimate citizenship: heaven.

Paul Knew Whom He Was Talking To

Paul knew how to appeal to the mind-set of his audience. He isn't being cavalier when he uses the metaphor of citizenship to picture our connection with heaven. He intentionally used that reference because it had special meaning to the Philippians. They took great pride in their Roman citizenship (and all the benefits that were afforded by it), so they could understand that citizens of heaven had certain privileges. Moreover, they were Roman citizens who were living in the outpost of the colony of Philippi; they could certainly understand the analogy of being citizens of heaven while living temporarily on earth.

If the Philippians needed any additional motivation to keep walking with Christ, a reminder of their ultimate destination ought to provide it. Despite whatever adversity may befall them while on earth, the Philippian Christians will end their spiritual sojourn with their arrival in heaven.

The antinomian philosophy has an attraction if you only consider your immediate circumstances. Living for the moment without any concern for the consequences has some appeal. But if you view life from an eternal perspective, then you'll immediately see that the antinomian approach is shortsighted. After all, life on earth has tragic downsides (especially if you are living with reckless abandon): The pleasures soon become unsatisfying; strife and stress, hatred and animosity, illness, pain, and disease all come our way; and ultimately we die. Contrast that with what awaits Christians when they are united with Christ. We will have new, spiritual bodies. The grunge of the earth will be behind us; we will have eternity to be with Christ. That should be the best motivation of all. As citizens of heaven, we will at last get to see Christ and know Him and enjoy His fellowship for eternity. Our Christian walk will have come to an end at the feet of Jesus.

> *Yes, dear friends, we are already God's children, and we can't even imagine what we will be like when Christ returns. But we do know that when he comes we will be like him, for we will see him as he really is* (1 John 3:2).

■ ■ ■

Study the Word

1. Becoming a Christian is simple. Maturing as a Christian is more difficult. It takes discipline. Read the following passages, in which Paul uses an athletic training metaphor for the Christian life: 1 Corinthians 9:24-27; 1 Timothy 4:7-10; 2 Timothy 4:7-8.

What does each of these passages add to what Paul said in Philippians 3:13-14?

2. Who is your Christian role model? What Christian traits have you learned from the person who serves as your example? If you don't have a Christian role model, what criteria should you be looking for in a person to fulfill this role?

3. Describe how your spiritual walk is going. Can you identify with Paul when he acknowledged that he was far from being perfect?

4. Which is easier: knowing (understanding) Christ or being like Him? How are the two related?

5. Paul laid out the prospect of being in heaven with Christ as motivation for continuing on in the Christian walk. Read Paul's description of this event in 1 Corinthians 15:51-54. Describe what you think being in God's presence in heaven will be like. Is this something you are looking forward to? Do you have any worries or hesitations about this?

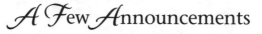 A Few Announcements

What if Martin Luther King, Jr., after giving his famous "I have a dream" speech, spent the next several minutes telling the crowd about the location of the porta-potties and the location of the buses for their return trips home? The juxtaposition of the inspirational speech with the mundane details would be perplexing. Well, get ready for it, because you're about to find that Paul concludes his letter to the Philippians in that fashion.

Many of Paul's letters end anticlimactically. In the opening chapters, he lays the foundation, and then he hammers on a particular point, crafting a literary crescendo that inspires the reader with the majesty of Christ. These peaks of inspiration usually make a perfect ending point, but Paul never stops there. Instead, he gets practical (and almost boring) with a few details and closing comments.

But don't be misled by the comments in Philippians 4 that seem comparatively dull at first glance. With his customary skill, Paul tucks away a few zingers in those verses which make them relevant not only for the Philippians but also for you.

Chapter 7

The Joy of Contentment

Philippians 4

*W*hat's *A*head

- [ ] Restoring Peace with Believers (4:1-3)

- [ ] Maintaining Focus on Christ (4:4-9)

- [ ] The Secret of Contentment (4:10-20)

- [ ] Final Greetings (4:21-23)

*T*his last chapter of Philippians is deceptively simple. In what appear to be some last-minute thoughts that he tags on to his letter, Paul artfully weaves together all of the themes that he emphasized earlier. It turns out to be an excellent way to reinforce the concepts of capturing the joy of Christianity in...

- harmonious relationships

- adverse circumstances

- an intimate walk with Christ

Restoring Peace with Believers (4:1-3)

After reading Philippians 4:1, you can't doubt that Paul had a special affection for the Philippians. By the way that he refers to them, he is showing that he considers them to be the best example of what his ministry was all about: establishing churches and seeing Christians grow in spiritual maturity with the Lord and each other.

Paul refers to the Philippian church as being his "crown" (NIV). It's a fashion accessory that isn't very popular today (except in beauty pageants), but a crown had great significance in the first century A.D. This reference would remind the Philippians of...

- *A victor's crown.* The winners of Greek games didn't receive a cash award, a trophy, or a medal. Their reward was a wreath of intertwined olive leaves. Although it seems modest, this "crown" was the ambition of every athlete because it acknowledged their accomplishment.

- *A guest's crown.* In what may have been the predecessor to the contemporary party hat, special guests at a banquet were often bestowed a crown for the evening. It signified their special role in the evening's festivities.

We don't know which analogy Paul had in mind. Maybe he considered himself to be an athlete on Christ's team, and the Philippians were the wreath that acknowledged his ministry. Maybe he was thinking about the festivities in heaven when we will be rejoicing with Christ, and the Philippian Christians will be the crown that symbolizes the cause for celebration.

Notice that Paul links his compliment of the Philippians with a caution to stay connected with the Lord. The Philippians had a strong and close relationship with the Lord; that was the reason Paul considered them to be his joy and crown. But they needed to keep working at that relationship. Your walk with the Lord can't be taken for granted. Like a relationship with any friend, it will deteriorate quickly if it is ignored. Paul didn't want the Philippians to be complacent or satisfied with their spiritual status quo. He wanted them to stay intimately connected with Christ, not because he is afraid of losing his "crown" but because he wants them to experience the joy of knowing Christ better.

Paul is undoubtedly writing sincerely as he compliments and encourages the Philippians in 4:1. But he may have a secondary motive for using these statements as a graceful way to broach a sensitive subject. Apparently, two women in the church couldn't get along with each other: Euodia and Syntyche. Paul doesn't mention the specifics of the rife, so they must have been obvious to everyone in the Philippian church. Consequently, we are spared the dramatic details. But Paul doesn't spare any intensity. He pleads with these women, by name, to settle their disagreement, and he directs the church to get involved in the process as well. From what Paul said earlier in 2:1-11, he knows that these women and the entire church are in danger of losing the joy of Christ if this friction continues.

Think About This

Euodia and Syntyche probably never expected that they would be remembered more than a generation or two after their deaths. But here we are, almost 2000 years later, and we are still talking about them. Unfortunately, all we know about them is that they were two bitter and quarreling women. That is a sad and sorry reputation to be attached to your name for 2000 years.

What if your reputation was reduced to a single sentence? How would your life and personality be characterized? Philippians gives you all of the basics you need to know if you are due for a personality overhaul.

Maintaining Focus on Christ (4:4-9)

If you had any doubt about Paul's theme for his letter to the Philippians, his statement at 4:4 ought to clear things up for you. This could be the theme verse for the entire letter. Having just mentioned the friction between Euodia and Syntyche, Paul doesn't want the Philippians to be distracted from the joy that comes from being in Christ, so he mentions it again. In fact, he says it twice in the same verse.

As he moves into the 4:6-9 passage, can you sense that Paul was on a roll that moves logically from joyfulness to spiritual tranquility? His next progression is equally obvious: If you have this spiritual tranquility, you shouldn't worry about anything. In other words, if God is in control (your basis of joy), then you can trust that He will take care of what you need.

You know enough about Paul to know that he wasn't a passive guy. He was proactive in all aspects of his life. You might sense a dichotomy between spiritual tranquility and being proactive in your Christian life. Well, Paul doesn't see one. He treats them as being compatible. Trusting God for our physical needs doesn't mean that we should be passive in this regard. (In other words, don't expect that God will provide your food and rent if you display your trust by quitting your job and spending all of your time watching reruns of *Touched by an Angel*.)

Paul isn't suggesting that you disengage from the practicalities of life because God has got you covered. But he is emphasizing that you shouldn't agonize over these things. Instead of generating excess stomach acid over your concerns, pray about them. Talk to God about your worries, thank Him for what He has done in the past, and thank Him for what He is going to do for you in the future.

Prayer is the way that we invoke God's involvement in our lives. More importantly, Paul adds, prayer is the way in which we remind ourselves that God is large and in charge. When we pray, we remind ourselves of who God is, and that understanding brings God's peace into our lives.

But staying focused on Christ is tricky when you are worried about the minor details of living (like food, clothing, and shelter). Experiencing Christ's joy is even harder when you are mentally occupied with thoughts and attitudes that are contrary to Christ's nature. Paul knows this, so he offers a solution: Keep your mind filled with thoughts that are consistent with Christ's nature. Here is his list of things to think about:

- things that are true

- things that are honorable

- things that are lovely, pure, and admirable

- things that are excellent and praiseworthy

Paul doesn't get more specific than that. With the Holy Spirit in the life of each Christian, we have an internal barometer on such matters. So we can apply this list to determine the appropriateness of our thoughts at any time, whether we are watching TV, surfing the Internet, reading a magazine, hanging out with friends, talking on the phone, or just daydreaming.

Paul knows from personal experience that these techniques don't come naturally or easily. They take practice. But he also knows from personal experience that when these principles are integrated into a believer's life, the peace of God will be evident.

The Secret of Contentment (4:10-20)

Did you lose sight of the fact that this was a thank-you letter from Paul to the Philippians? Paul didn't. And even though he thanked them at the beginning of the letter for supporting him and being his partners in ministry (1:5-7), he does so again in these concluding comments.

Paul loves the Philippians, but not because he viewed them as an ATM. Sure, he was grateful for their financial support, but his affection was premised on their devotion to Christ. This is an important distinction that he wants them to understand:

- He appreciates their concern for him.

- Sometimes they were able to send money to him, and he is grateful for that.

- But other times they were unable to send anything to him. When this happened, he never questioned their commitment to him.

- Of all the churches with which he was associated, the Philippians were his most loyal supporters—spiritually as well as financially.

Paul didn't want them to think that this discussion about his appreciation for their financial support was a disguised plea for more money. So he tells them that money isn't really important. In making his point, Paul pens two of his most famous verses. They are buried away at the end of his Philippian letter in this discussion of financial support, but they reveal the secret of how Paul manages to find joy in his life regardless of his circumstances:

- First, he says he knows a secret to contentment: *"I have learned the secret of living in every situation"* (4:12).

- Then, he reveals the secret: *"I can do everything with the help of Christ who gives me the strength I need"* (4:13).

Paul didn't say that wealth was bad, and he didn't say that poverty was close to godliness. He had lived in both conditions. He was saying that he was contented either way. He knew that God was in control. That thought alone brought him great joy, so his surrounding circumstances suddenly became irrelevant.

Try It Yourself

If you find that you are worrying more than rejoicing, perhaps you are assuming too much responsibility for your life. Let God take control. Relinquish the responsibility for those problems to God. Relax in the fact that He is capable to handle them. Rejoice in the knowledge that He'll do a better job with the details of your life than you ever could.

Final Greetings (4:21-23)

The final, friendly greetings at the end of the letter are self-explanatory, with one exception. Notice the reference to Caesar's household. Paul isn't suggesting that Caesar's kids and relatives were fans of the Philippian Christians. The Christians in Philippi knew that Paul was talking about the Christians who were working in positions of the government. Of course, Paul couldn't reveal any names due to reprisals from Caesar, but some Christians must have been employed as Caesar's secretaries, soldiers, financial officers, and administrators. Knowing that the influence of Christ was permeating the operation of the Roman Empire was a definite cause of rejoicing.

And so the letter ends. It started with Paul's statement that his imprisonment has advanced the Gospel (1:12) and ended with the reference that proves it (4:22). Perhaps this was the best illustration that adversity is of no consequence when you experience the joy of knowing Christ and seeing Him at work in the details of your life.

■ ■ ■

Study the Word

1. Now that you've studied the entire book of Philippians, give a definition for *Christian joy*. (Go ahead, make Paul proud.)

2. Paul encouraged the members of the church in Philippi to get involved in bringing Euodia and Syntyche to a place of reconciliation in their relationship. What are some practical steps that you can take when you have two Christian friends who are angry at each other?

3. What does Paul mean when he says: "Don't worry about anything" (4:6)? Is that possible? Is it practical?

4. Our culture is filled with distractions that are far from wholesome. How can we live in the world but keep our minds focused on Christ? What are some ways in which we can keep our minds on the things that Paul identifies in 4:8?

5. Have you gotten to the point where you are content in any situation? If you are struggling with anxiety over something, what is the best way to get rid of it?

Let's Get Technical

As you move from Philippians to Colossians, a lot more will shift than just the bookmark in your Bible. The primary subject of both books (Christ) is the same, and the author (Paul) is the same, but just about everything else changes. Nonetheless, these two books make good study companions.

In Philippians, Paul gave practical advice about living the Christian life. In the course of explaining how it is done, he wove in some good theology about Christ.

In writing to the Colossians, Paul's primary purpose is to explain some technical points of theology and doctrine about Christ. As he does so, he explains how this knowledge ought to affect a Christian's everyday life.

Both books involve theology and the practicalities of real life, but they come at those subjects from different directions.

At the first reading, Colossians might seem too heavy on the theology side. For this reason, many people think that the message of Philippians is more relevant than Colossians. After all, everybody deals with problems, tough times, and adversities (Philippians), but most of us don't find ourselves engaged in deep doctrinal debates (Colossians). But that's exactly what Satan wants you to think—that you don't have to worry about theology because you don't have much occasion to use it. As you're about to read, the lessons of Colossians are perhaps more culturally relevant now than ever.

Chapter 8

Colossians: Big Thoughts to a Small Church

What's Ahead

- [ ] Not Much to Brag About

- [ ] A Brouhaha Brewing

- [ ] So What's in It for You?

Colossians is a rare "To Whom It May Concern" letter from Paul. Paul customarily wrote to people that he knew well (such as his protégé, Timothy, in the letters of 1 and 2 Timothy) or to churches that he established (like Philippians). Paul wrote Colossians and Romans to people at churches that he had nothing to do with. But that fact ought to pique your curiosity. What was so important that Paul was compelled to write a letter to people he didn't know?

Not Much to Brag About

The letter to the Colossians certainly wasn't motivated by Paul's desire to finagle a business trip to the city of Colosse. It was not a destination hot spot of the first century A.D. From all historical accounts, it was a city on the decline. But it hadn't always been that way.

Colosse was located in the Lycus Valley (located in modern-day Turkey) on the major thoroughfare from Italy and Greece to Syria and Mesopotamia. Together with its neighboring cities of Laodicea and Hierapolis, Colosse came under Roman rule in 133 B.C., but each city was allowed some autonomy in its civic affairs. The chief industry of this region was the manufacture of woolen fabrics.

Of these three cities, Colosse was the oldest and most prominent—for a while. In what must have been a battle among the Chambers of Commerce, Laodicea and Hierapolis started to pull ahead and leave Colosse in the dust (literally):

- By the first century A.D., the economic prosperity of Laodicea had surpassed Colosse's. The combination of being famous for the fine, black wool of its sheep and its strategic location at the intersection of a highway system put Laodicea on the map. The factors of trade, commerce, banking, and riches suddenly made Laodicea the political capital of the region.

- Hierapolis became a resort town. Volcanic activity produced hot springs in this city, and thousands of people journeyed to Hierapolis each year to enjoy the "healing waters" of its spas. Lots of superstitions were associated with these hot springs, and many pagan religious temples were constructed in the area. The name *Hierapolis* means "the holy city." That may reveal the mystic importance that people placed on these deep springs.

By the time Paul wrote this letter (around A.D. 60), Colosse was being passed over for Laodicea and Hierapolis. If you were looking for pleasure and a relaxing time, you headed for Hierapolis; if you were more interested in politics and money, then Laodicea was your place. But the dwindling population of Colosse stayed in their city because someone had to live there.

No wonder Paul never visited Colosse. But he did have the opportunity to meet some individuals from the Colossian church:

- Epaphras was a leader in the Colossian church. He was visiting Paul in Rome during Paul's imprisonment, and Epaphras' report on the condition of things back in Colosse prompted Paul to write his letter.

- A Christian slave, Onesimus, belonged to the Colossian church. Onesimus ran away from his owner, Philemon, and ended up in Rome visiting "guess who" in jail. Paul's letter to Philemon (asking that he accept Onesimus back as his Christian brother) reveals that Paul knew both of these men. The Colossian church may have met in Philemon's home.

- Paul also knew Archippus (who some scholars believe to be the son of Philemon). Archippus held some sort of leadership role in the church at Colosse.

If Not Paul, Then Who?

Scholars are certain that Paul didn't start the church in Colosse. Some theorize that Epaphras, a hometown boy of Colosse, was visiting the big city of Ephesus during the three-year period that Paul lived and preached there. They believe that Epaphras became a Christian while in Ephesus and then returned home, where he shared the Gospel message with his friends and family. Before long, a small group of believers formed in Colosse, and from those humble beginnings, the Colossian church was born. With such apparent spiritual responsibility for the Christians in Colosse, Epaphras would be likely to travel to visit Paul in Rome if Epaphras was worried about the spiritual welfare of his church family.

If this is how the church started, then no traveling missionary or famous evangelist ever set foot in Colosse; the church just happened as the natural outgrowth of one person sharing his faith with others. What does that suggest to you about your ability to spread Christ's message in your community?

A Brouhaha Brewing

The Lycus Valley was a veritable smorgasbord of religious and spiritual beliefs. The Christians were the late arrivals. This region had long been influenced by the philosophies and mythologies of the Greeks and Romans. Added to the mix was the pagan worship that arose in Hierapolis. A significant Jewish population in the Lycus Valley was mostly integrally involved in the dyed wool and related trades in Laodicea (but also attracted by the hot-water spas of Hierapolis). So the prevailing religious philosophies bombarding the Christians came from two sources: paganism and Judaism.

Paul had received a report, most likely from Epaphras, that the Colossian Christians were hearing false teachings. Paul was concerned that they would be swayed by the fallacies of what has become known as the Colossian heresy. Apparently, a sect of religious teachers in the Lycus Valley had blended together a spiritual recipe that looked attractive on the superficial level but actually undercut the basis of the Gospel.

Interestingly, Paul didn't go into great detail in articulating the points of the false doctrine. He didn't have to; the Colossians knew what he was talking about. (More importantly, Paul wanted to spend his time talking about the truth, not the lie.) But from references in his letters and historical accounts, the Colossian heresy appears to have had the following elements:

- At its core, Paul was dealing with a form of gnosticism. Its proponents claimed a superior knowledge and esoteric wisdom ("gnosis"). They claimed that knowing God was possible only through this higher level of intellectualism.

- Gnosticism had some appeal because the paganism and immorality in the region was so prevalent. The gnostics made a big distinction between the goodness of God and the evil in the world. Consequently, they argued, God could not be connected with the material world. Levels of increasing spirituality ("emanations") must lead from earth to God.

- The gnostics didn't completely reject Jesus, but they taught that Jesus couldn't be the means of salvation. They contended that Jesus couldn't be God because Jesus lived on earth. So, they opined, either Jesus was not a true man (and was some form of angel), or He was a man (but not God) who was on some lower rung of the emanation ladder and who had the Spirit of God hovering over Him from the time of His baptism until His crucifixion.

- The Colossian heresy had a little bit of Judaism thrown in for good measure. The Jewish regulations, particularly those referring to circumcision and dietary restrictions, were necessary for moving up to the higher levels of thought.

- Paul also suggests that the heresy included angel worship (which would be logical if Jesus was reduced to the level of an angel).

- Finally, for the hard-core types who really wanted to feel like they had done something extra to earn their salvation, the heresy included a sprinkling of asceticism (with all of its austere lifestyle that repudiated the excesses of hedonism).

For the most part, the elements of the Colossian heresy don't seem too bad: an increased focus on knowing God, a distinction between good and evil, ceremonies that reinforce spiritual principles, prohibitions against immorality. Yes, these are all good things—unless they erode the fundamental principle of Christianity: Jesus Christ alone is our means of salvation.

The Colossian heresy used a ploy that can be quite deceiving. It took certain elements of the truth and then added something, subtracted a few things, and bent any portion of the truth that remained. By starting from a position of truth, the heresy can sound good. But the revisions of the truth make the heresy spiritually fatal.

Paul Is Worried but Not Ticked Off

In the letter to the Galatians, Paul doesn't hide the fact that he is annoyed that the Christians in Galatia were buying into the teaching of false doctrine. Paul isn't as harsh with the Colossians. Maybe this is because Paul taught in the church in Galatia, so he felt they should know better. The Colossians, however, were a church of Christians who were younger in their faith. So Paul takes a different approach with the Colossians.

His opponents (the gnostics) had apparently issued a critique of the Gospel as preached by Paul. He accepts the challenge by affirming the Colossians' faithfulness, and then he proceeds to dissect the opposition point by point.

So What's in It for You?

You might be wondering whether Colossians is relevant for you. You've probably never had occasion to debate the distinctions of gnosticism with anyone. Well, the labels may be different, but you are in exactly the same place the Colossians were in 20 centuries ago.

You are living in a culture that offers a smorgasbord of religious opinions. To be sure, Christianity is on the buffet line, but so are many other belief systems. People are picking and choosing what they want to put on their spiritual plate. Unfortunately, many people are convinced that they can pick and choose little bits from many different religions and end up with a religion that is suitable for their personal tastes. The Colossians were dealing with the blended views of gnosticism; you are living in a culture that is dominated by religious pluralism—the view that any religion is the right one so long as it is right for you.

Your study of Colossians will teach you about the supremacy of Jesus Christ. After all, that's how you spot a heresy. The central issue is always Jesus. How do people deal with Him? Is He God or something less? Is belief in Him the only way to obtain salvation, or do you have to do something else?

If you want to be able to articulate your faith in a culture that is predisposed to believe that all religions are the same, you've got to know what you believe. And if you are a Christian, then you've got to know about Jesus. So, read through the entire book of Colossians before you get to the study of the specific passages that begin in the next chapter. Don't worry, the entire letter of Colossians is only 94 verses long. As you do this initial read-through, be on the lookout for:

- references to the deity and uniqueness of Jesus Christ

- discussions about Christ's death on the cross accomplishing the complete work of salvation

- counterarguments to asceticism in which Paul proclaims the liberty and freedom that we enjoy as Christians

Jesus said that you are to "love the Lord your God with all your heart, all your soul, and all your mind" (Matthew 22:37). Colossians is all about using your mind to think through the importance of Jesus Christ. The more we understand who Christ is and what He did for us, the more we'll love Him—and the better equipped we'll be to refute heresies that seek to undermine Him.

■ ▢ ▣

Study the Word

1. Why was Paul so concerned about the spiritual beliefs of the people in Colosse, most of whom he had never met?

2. Paul wasn't worried that the Colossians would switch religions. His concern was that they'd adopt some screwy views under the mistaken impression that these false teachings were doctrines of Christianity. Review what you know about the Colossian heresy. What are some of the ways that people try to bend the truth of Christianity today?

3. Can all religions be correct? (Hint: Each major religion of the world contends that its doctrine is the truth and that other religions are wrong.) How can a study of Colossians be helpful to you in combating the false notions of religious pluralism?

4. Make a checklist of the things that you believe about Christ. Make this list as exhaustive as possible. Save this list and review it when you have completed your study of Colossians to see if your understanding of Christ has changed.

5. The Christians in Colosse were entertaining the beliefs of other people. What does this fact suggest to you about: (a) the importance of selecting your friends and (b) the importance of knowing what you believe?

*E*mphasize the *P*ositive...

Child psychologists recommend that you say something positive to children before you criticize their behavior. This makes sense. A complimentary preface establishes a rapport so the child isn't on the defensive at the outset. Criticism is always easier to accept if it can be balanced by compliments.

Paul employs this same strategy in his letter to the Colossian Christians. He won't be criticizing them in the letter, but he will be challenging their thinking. And they might have trembled a bit as the letter was opened and read for the first time, wondering if they were going to get yelled at by the world's most famous missionary. So Paul begins his letter by putting everyone at ease. As you read the first 14 verses of Colossians 1, you'll understand that Paul had reason to be proud of these Christians. They had grasped the truth of the Gospel, and their lives showed it. Paul sincerely believes that, and he wants to reinforce it at the very beginning of his letter.

Watch for the traits that Paul sees in the lives of the Colossians that flow naturally from their knowledge of the truth of the Gospel. Are these same traits evident in your life?

Chapter 9

Knowing the Truth
of the Gospel

Colossians 1:1-14

What's Ahead

- More than a Standard Greeting (1:1-2)

- Thankfulness for Who They Are (1:3-8)

- Praying for Who They Will Become (1:9-14)

The letter of Colossians was written to the entire church, not just an individual. Although it was hand-carried to Colosse, a church leader probably didn't open it in the privacy of his home. This was a letter from the world's most famous missionary. This small church, in this boring town, probably never expected to get such a letter. This was a big deal. A huge deal. Most probably, a special meeting of the church family was convened for the specific purpose of reading this letter aloud so everyone could hear it at the same time. Imagine their anticipation as the parchment was unwrapped and someone began reading. Imagine their relief as they heard the warm and encouraging words of this first passage.

More Than a Standard Greeting (1:1-2)

Paul customarily identified himself as an *apostle*. This was an important designation. The original group of 12 apostles were the men who were with Christ during His earthly ministry, saw Him face-to-face, spent time with Him, saw His miracles, and knew Him intimately. (The other people who followed Christ—and those of us who continue to follow Him—are called *disciples*.) Even though Paul wasn't part of that original group of 12, he was recognized as an apostle because he satisfied similar criteria:

- He saw the risen Christ in his conversion experience on the road to Damascus (Acts 9:1-19; 1 Corinthians 9:1; 15:8-9).

- He possessed miraculous powers that God gave to the apostles to authenticate them (2 Corinthians 12:12; Hebrews 2:3-4).

Paul wasn't being egotistical about this. In fact, he says that God chose him to be an apostle; Paul didn't campaign for the position. Although everyone knew he was an apostle, he reminded the Colossians about it. He wanted to substantiate his authority to refute the false teachings of the gnostics. None of them could claim this title.

Paul frequently names a companion in the beginning of the letter. As in the letter to the Philippians, Paul mentions that Timothy is with him.

Paul addresses the letter to the Christians in the church at Colosse, but he does it more eloquently than that. He refers to them with these descriptive and meaningful terms:

- Paul refers to them as a holy people. They were consecrated ("set apart") as God's people. This was not due to anything special that they had done. Rather, because they responded to God's calling, He did a divine transformation in their lives.

- Paul acknowledges their faithfulness. He knew they were well intentioned in their belief. They wanted to be faithful to the truth (but they just needed a little additional information to refute the false teachings of the gnostics).

- Paul includes them as part of his close, intimate spiritual family. Just as he referred to Timothy as a brother (1:1), he calls the Colossian Christians his brothers and sisters.

- Paul emphasizes that all of these characteristics stem from a relationship "in Christ." (He is setting the stage for the arguments he'll begin to make in 1:15 and following.)

Paul concludes his greeting with his common practice of pronouncing a blessing of God's grace (His lovingkindness that we don't deserve) and God's peace (the calm that can only be experienced by a Christian who knows that Christ has restored his relationship with God).

Thankfulness for Who They Are (1:3-8)

Even though Paul doesn't know the Colossians, he knows about them. And what he knows causes him to be thankful to God. Why to God? Shouldn't he be thankful to the Colossians? (After all, they are the ones whose behavior is what Paul appreciates.) The answer is found in the passage itself. Paul says that the Colossians knew the truth of the Gospel. The Gospel (the "Good News" about Christ) was what changed their lives. Thus, Paul's thankfulness is directed to God because His truth brought about the transformation.

Just how, exactly, did their knowledge of the truth of the Gospel change their lives? To make sure that they realized it themselves, Paul gives them the three-part answer. Knowledge of the truth about God produced three things in them:

1. ***Faith in Jesus Christ.*** Don't let the significance of this simple statement slip by you. Remember that the Colossian heresy taught that much more was required than just faith. False teachers told the Colossians that rituals and regulations—and a higher intellectual level of thinking—were also prerequisites to salvation. But Paul considers those things nonessentials. All that is necessary is faith in Jesus Christ, and the Colossians have a lock on that.

2. ***Love for other Christians.*** True Christianity is not limited to a love of Christ. That's a given, but the real test is whether a Christian has a love for other people. (Let's face it. Jesus is a lot easier to love than the people we come in contact with.) Loving other Christians should be as natural as loving Christ. This was a hallmark of the early Christian church, and it was a command that Christ gave to His disciples (John 13:34-35).

3. ***Hope for the future in heaven.*** This kind of hope is not like a wish or a desire (as in "I hope I get a big inheritance someday"). In this context, *hope* means the certainty that comes from our faith. As

Christians, the Colossians could depend on the knowledge that their future was going to bring them into the presence of God Almighty.

Faith, love, and hope share an interesting interconnection. Our faith considers the work of Christ in the past and causes us to look upward toward God; our love involves present action on our part and causes us to look outward to others; and our hope anticipates the future and causes us to look forward to Christ's return. Faith, love, and hope: These are natural characteristics that flow from knowing the truth of the Gospel.

How Did Paul Know All This Stuff?

For a guy who never visited Colosse and was only acquainted with two or three members of the church, Paul sure seems to know a lot about the Colossian Christians. The reason why is found in 1:7-8. Epaphras, the one who brought the Gospel to his hometown of Colosse, went to visit Paul, and he was apparently with Paul during the writing of this letter.

Praying for Who They Will Become (1:9-14)

Paul has just explained that he prays with thankfulness for the spiritual character that the Colossian Christians display. But he wants to move them into deeper maturity, so next he describes his prayers for their spiritual growth.

Basically, Paul is praying for two things for the Colossians:

- First, he is praying that they may be able to discern God's will. The Christian's task is to pursue God's will. We just can't sit back and let things happen and say "Well, that must be God's will" with a fatalistic attitude. To the contrary, we should proactively pursue the path that God has for us. Most Christians will say that this is not easy. As Paul's prayer indicates, how much you know about God's will is determined by how well you know God.

- Secondly, Paul is praying that they may have the power to perform God's will. Knowing God's will is of little value unless you are going to act on what you know. But the accomplishment of God's will requires more than human strength. It requires God's supernatural power.

Do you ever wonder what you should pray for? Maybe Paul's prayer can be a helpful model for you. As Paul did for the Colossians, you can pray for the *knowledge* of what God wants you to do and the *power* to do it.

Within the context of those two prayer requests, Paul identifies six characteristics that will be present in the lives of the Colossians as they grow in spiritual maturity:

1. ***They'll understand God's will.*** How this happens is no secret. The keys are knowledge and spiritual wisdom. Knowledge is familiarity with biblical principles. Spiritual wisdom is the ability to use that knowledge as a basis for making good choices. When you consider the circumstances of your life from God's perspective, His will becomes more apparent.

2. ***They will honor God by the way they live.*** We can't please God if we are walking in a direction that is opposite from the way He wants us to go.

Often referred to as "walking in a worthy manner," this characteristic refers to a lifestyle that is consistent with godly behavior.

3. *Their lives will be spiritually productive.* Knowing God's will and honoring Him with our actions will naturally result in acts of service. This represents a Christian life that is "fruitful." (Agricultural analogies were big in Bible times.) Note that this behavior is not dictated or required as a condition of salvation. Rather, it should be a natural expression in our lives as we know God better and seek to please Him.

4. *Their knowledge of God will continue to increase.* A stagnant Christian life has a static knowledge of God. A growing Christian, in contrast, keeps gaining greater insights into God's nature. This does not mean that you abandon truth that you learned previously; you simply add to it. Like the roots and branches of a tree, your knowledge of God grows deeper and wider.

5. *Their spiritual character will be strengthened.* Two signs of stronger character are endurance (long-suffering) and patience. Endurance is the ability to handle difficult circumstances. Patience is the ability to deal with difficult people.

6. *They will experience joy and thankfulness.* If you've already studied Philippians, you know about joy. It isn't a superficial happiness. It is peace that comes from knowing that you're loved by God and that He is in charge. That realization automatically produces an attitude of gratefulness.

These are the characteristics that Paul prayed would be present in the lives of the Christians in Colosse. But they aren't exclusive to the Colossians. If you are a growing Christian who seeks to be more mature in your faith, then you should have these same characteristics.

Being Spiritual in the Here and Now

As he concluded this passage, Paul was probably thinking about the false teaching of the gnostics. They preached that salvation required higher levels of understanding. Perhaps Paul doesn't want the Colossian Christians to misunderstand what he has just said about spiritual maturity and growing in the knowledge of God. So, unlike the gnostics, who pontificated higher levels of intellectualism and mumbo jumbo mysticism, Paul wants to connect the real life with the spiritual life. He does so by referring to two kingdoms: God's kingdom and Satan's realm, light and dark, good and evil, the spirit and the flesh. The gnostics, by the way, also believed in the existence of these two kingdoms. But, contrary to their view, Paul emphasizes that Christians are presently citizens of God's kingdom, and we have been from the moment of our salvation, thanks to Christ's death on the cross. Deeper knowledge of God doesn't give us salvation, but it gives us an understanding of how God wants us to live.

Study the Word

1. Suppose Paul was writing a letter to you based on information that he had been given by one of your Christian friends. What would be the things in your life that would make him thankful to God? In what areas might he pray for you to grow?

2. Identify someone you know whose life appears to bring honor to God. What specific things about this person made you identify him or her? List some attitudes as well as actions.

3. "Faith, hope, and love" are a favorite trilogy of Paul's. Read 1 Thessalonians 1:3 and 1 Peter 1:3,5,22 for other instances in which Paul refers to the combination of these traits. Next read 1 Corinthians 13. Which of these three does Paul consider the greatest? Why do you think he holds that opinion?

4. Christians usually want to know God's will for their lives. They often mistakenly believe that God's will involves a certain place, person, or activity. What does Paul say (in 1:9-11) is necessary for knowing God's will? What additional insights can you gain from what Paul said in Romans 12:2?

5. Explain how the passage of Colossians 1:1-14 can be used as a guideline for praying on behalf of (a) yourself, (b) your friends, and (c) other Christians that you may not know personally (such as missionaries).

The Content Is Concentrated

You might wonder why chapter 10 covers only nine verses. (If we prorated all of the verses of Colossians equally among chapters 9–13—which we obviously haven't done—then we'd cover 19 verses per chapter.)

The answer is simple. The nine verses of Colossians 1:15-23 contain more than any of us can handle. What you are about to read is considered by many Bible scholars to be the most concise, yet deep, theological treatise on the person, deity, and work of Jesus Christ.

Imagine that! You are about to read a treasured passage that is likely to expand your understanding of who Christ is. From this point forward, you'll think about Christ in a new way. That knowledge is likely to change your life forever because you'll have even greater confidence in the One you call your Savior.

Chapter 10

Knowing the Supremacy of Christ

Colossians 1:15-23

*W*hat's *A*head

- ☐ Christ's Role as God (1:15)
- ☐ Christ's Role in the Universe (1:15-17)
- ☐ Christ's Role in Redemption (1:18-20)
- ☐ Christ's Role in Your Life (1:21-23)

*I*n this chapter you'll be studying Paul's response to the gnostics, which blows them out of the debate. Of course, the Colossians knew each and every point of gnosticism that Paul refuted in his discussion about Christ. You don't have to be an expert in ancient heresies to appreciate this passage, but a brief overview of the Colossian heresy might give you a better context for understanding what Paul is about to say. Here are some of the major points of the Colossian heresy in a nutshell:

- The gnostics ("the intellectual ones") thought that Christianity was too simplistic. After all, anyone could understand it. Certainly God intended it to have a sophistication equal to other philosophies of the time.

- Start with the premise that matter is totally evil, and the spirit is totally good. Both are eternal. Since the world is matter, it was created out of evil matter.

- God is all spirit and therefore totally good, so He couldn't have been involved in creation of an evil world. God must have created layers of lesser beings or powers, each progressively further removed from Him. The last in this series of "emanations" was so far removed from God that it could touch matter, and it created the world. (Thus, this lowest-rung emanation created the world, God didn't.)

- The gnostics considered Jesus to be one of the emanations. He might have been on one of the higher rungs, but He was still just one of God's lackeys (like the many other emanations). Jesus wasn't God.

- But Jesus wasn't a man either. The body of man is matter, and matter is evil. Consequently, a high-ranking emanation of the totally good God, such as Jesus, couldn't ever be ensconced in an evil physical body. Jesus couldn't have been real flesh and blood, so He must have been a spiritual phantom in a bodily form (which is why, according to gnostic belief, Jesus left no footprints when He walked on the ground).

- God can't ever reach down to humanity. (Remember, He can't touch evil.) So humanity's job is to find God. But you can't get to Him directly. You've got to go through those infinite layers of emanations. Each level required special knowledge (the ancient equivalent of a password). This means that salvation required specialized knowledge, and it wasn't available to everyone (because most people, except the gnostics, were mental buffoons).

As man-made religious systems go, this one isn't too bad. At least it has a logical flow. But as with all man-made religions—or variations on Christianity—it ignores the truth about God and Jesus, as Paul is about to explain.

Christ's Role as God (1:15)

Christ is no diluted version of God. He is no distant emanation of God. Jesus is God. So much so, that if you see Jesus, you have seen God. He is the Real Deal. This is what Paul means when he says that Jesus is the visible image of the invisible God. Jesus Himself said the same thing:

> *Anyone who has seen me has seen the Father!*
> (John 14:9).

Don't be thrown by the word *image*. Paul is not suggesting that Christ gives us a rough idea of God (like a police artist's drawing). Paul's use of that term implies that Jesus is the exact and complete manifestation of God. Jesus does not fall short of God the Father in any way; God the Father has no characteristics that were not embodied in Christ. They are the same in all respects. But it is even more than that. Jesus is not just equal to God—He is God.

*K*eep *C*olossians 1:15 *H*andy

This verse was obviously helpful to the Colossian Christians in rebutting the philosophy of the gnostics, but can you see how this verse is useful to you? In any religious discussion, you can immediately spot a false teaching if someone places Christ in any role or position other than God.

Christ's Role in the Universe (1:15-17)

If Christ is the exact image of God, then He must have always been so. God is eternal (He has always existed) and so is Christ. He was not created by God—He always existed as God. This is the same point that the apostle John made when He referred to Christ as *the Word:*

> *In the beginning the Word already existed. He was with God, and he was God. He was in the beginning with God* (John 1:1-2).

Paul calls Jesus the "firstborn" over all creation (NIV). By this reference, Paul doesn't mean that Jesus was born. (Jesus had no point of beginning. That doesn't happen when you are eternal and outside time and space.) Paul is using *firstborn* in the royal sense of a prince—the first-born male child of a king. Just like a prince, Christ has full dominion and authority over everything in the kingdom. In God's case, the kingdom is all of creation.

Speaking of creation (do you like Paul's segue?), the universe was not created by an emanation far removed by God. In God's plan, Jesus put the whole universe into place. You've probably heard of the principle of cause and effect (for every effect, there has to be something that caused it). The existence of the universe is the effect, and Jesus was the Cause that made it happen.

Notice that Christ's involvement with the universe covers both the material and the spiritual world. He created everything that you can see and also everything in the spiritual world that operates outside the sphere of our senses. When Paul mentions "authorities," he is referring to the spirit world and the hierarchy of angels and demons—all of which are under Christ's dominion.

Many Greco-Roman philosophers said that Zeus held all things in the universe together. Paul wants to emphasize that the unifying force in the cosmos is Christ. He is the sustainer of the universe; it is held together by and for Him. The so-called scientific laws that keep our universe orderly and functioning—such as the law of gravity—are really divine laws under Christ's control.

Getting Personal

These principles about Christ's involvement in the universe have direct application to your life. The world is not here by chance or some random confluence of cosmological circumstances. The world was created by Christ. And your life is not a meaningless happenstance of biological evolution. Everything in the world—including you—was created by Christ and is subject to His control. As a Christian, you should never despair about the events of the world or your place in it. Your Savior is the One who is in charge of the world and all that happens in the universe.

Christ's Role in Redemption (1:18-20)

Not only is Christ the Creator and Ruler of the universe, He is the centerpiece of the church—the universal fellowship of all believers who have accepted Christ as Savior. Paul sets out four great aspects of Christ's relationship to His body of believers:

Christ Is the Head of the Church

The analogy is to a physical body, with all of the parts subject to the control and direction of the head (brain). And so it is with the church. All action should be subject to the direction of Christ. And to take the analogy further, just as the head does the thinking for the body, so too our Head (Christ) is the source of our truth.

Christ Is the First of the Church

This characterization has several meanings. He was the first in the sense of time. The church didn't come into existence until Christ's death on the cross. Christ is also first in the sense that He is the source of life for the church. Only His death and resurrection can bring us into eternal life. Finally, Christ was the first to have resurrected life. All Christians will enjoy a resurrection too, but it is delayed until Christ's return.

Christ Is First Among Things

Because Christ is supreme in the universe and first in the spiritual sense, He has and deserves supremacy in all things. (Although we are quick to acknowledge Christ's supremacy in the universal and spiritual realms, we are often slow to give Him first place in our personal lives. We dishonor His authority when we preclude Him from taking first place in our thoughts, conversations, and activities.)

Christ Is the Fullness of God

This reference connects with the statement in 1:15 that Christ is the image of God. To refute any gnostic notion that Jesus was not human and divine at the same time, Paul says that the fullness of God lived in Jesus, in a physical body that bled on the cross. (See also Colossians 2:9.)

These factors provide the basis for Christ's work of redemption (saving us from our sins). The goal of this death on the cross was to reconcile us to Him. Our sins cut us off from an intimate relationship with Him, but His death covered the penalty for our sins, so we can be made right with Him and enjoy fellowship with Him.

Notice three important points in verse 20. First, we are reconciled to God; He is not reconciled to us. After all, our sin cut us off from God. We need to be brought back to a right relationship with Him. Secondly, Christ's death on the cross was a work of reconciliation for more than just us; it extends to everything in heaven and on earth. In other words, all of nature will be restored as God intended it from the beginning because Christ's death will eventually erase the effects of sin. But thirdly, the work of redemption and reconciliation does not extend to things under the earth as Satan and his demons continue in their rebellion.

Christ's Role in Your Life (1:21-23)

Okay, you aren't mentioned specifically in this passage. But you might as well be. Everything that Paul says about the Colossian Christians is true for you. In fact, when you come to the word *you* in this passage, read it as if Paul has *you* in mind. Reading the passage from that perspective, Paul is saying that...

- In the past you were cut off from Christ because of your sin. Your thoughts and actions were opposed to Him. Even though you might have been a nice person, you were living in rebellion. He was supreme, but you would not live in submission to Him.

- All of this changed when you accepted Him as your Savior. Although you're not yet perfect, your sins were forgiven because of His death on the cross. He endured agonizing physical pain for you. He was not some spiritual phantom that died a symbolic death. The blood He shed for you was real.

- By reason of your redemption, you have been reconciled with Him to a place of intimate friendship.

- God sees you as perfect and holy (because your past, present, and future sins have been forgiven).

But Paul doesn't stop there. He wants you to stand firm in your understanding and commitment to these truths. Don't waver or doubt what you know. Don't be persuaded to believe something different by false teachings that deviate from these biblical principles.

■ ▨ ▢

Study the Word

1. Review the list of gnostic beliefs on pages 111–113. How is each of those points refuted by Paul's presentation of Christ in Colossians 1:15-23?

2. What does Paul mean when he says that Christ is the "visible image" of God? What about the phrase "For God in all his fullness was pleased to live in Christ"? What are the implications of those two statements?

3. Spiritually speaking, what is the difference between *redemption* and *reconciliation?* Why is each of them important to a Christian?

4. Why is the deity of Christ a fundamental principle of Christianity? What happens to Christianity if you take the position that Jesus was not God? Now switch it around. Why is the humanity of Christ a fundamental principle of Christianity? What happens to Christianity if you take the position that Jesus was not human?

5. Some contemporary religions and cults seek to reduce Christ to a prophet or a wise teacher. Describe how your knowledge of Christ's supremacy can give you greater confidence in life than would be possible if Christ were someone less than God.

The Genuine Article

Congratulations. With that last chapter, you studied one of the heaviest theological discussions in the entire Bible. (By the way, don't think you've got it mastered. Keep reading Colossians 1:15-23 as you continue to mature in your faith. Each time you read it you'll gain further insights about our wonderful Christ. The words won't change, but they'll have greater meaning for you.)

Having explained the supremacy of Christ in all things, Paul now seeks to integrate that principle into the worldview of Colossian Christians. He wants them to evaluate everything from that perspective. In particular, Paul wants them to be able to analyze the fallacies of the gnostic doctrines on their own. He knows they'll need to focus on the truth of Christ in order to expose the deception of false teaching.

This is a bit like trying to spot counterfeit currency. FBI agents don't study fake currency; there are too many fraudulent variations to know each one (and new fakes are turning up all the time.) Instead, they study the genuine article. By knowing what a real bill looks like, they can more easily spot a fake.

And so it is with our Christian faith. When we understand the supremacy and all-sufficiency of Christ, and when we know Him well enough, we'll be able to spot false teachings. Paul knew this would work for the Colossian Christians, and it can work for you.

Chapter 11

Knowing the Deception of Counterfeit Truth

Colossians 1:24–2:23

*W*hat's *A*head

- Mystery Solved (1:24-29)
- The Characteristics of Faith Based on Truth (2:1-7)
- Using the Truth to Spot Deception (2:8-23)

*D*on't forget that Paul was writing this letter from prison. He was awaiting trial before Nero. The outcome of the trial was uncertain, but execution was a very real possibility. Imagine Paul's heartache for these young Colossian Christians. He may not be around much longer to protect them from religious charlatans. This letter may be the last opportunity to give them the tools for identifying false teachings.

Rather than just hammer on the points he wants to make, Paul gracefully moves into the subject of spotting counterfeit truth by sharing his passion for ministry—and his compassion for the Christians in Colosse.

Mystery Solved (1:24-29)

From your study thus far in Philippians and Colossians, you know Paul pretty well. Well enough, at least, to understand his love for Christ and his compassion for other believers. So, you might not be shocked by the first few verses in this passage. However, a reader without your background might think that Paul is equating his sufferings with the afflictions that Christ endured (1:24). But you know he must mean something different than that, and so he does. Paul is conveying the concept that his hardships are merely the extension of troubles and sufferings that are associated with being a Christian and spreading the Gospel. This happens when you identify yourself with Christ. The world hated Christ and persecuted Him (to the point of killing Him). The people of the world haven't gotten any better, so they will naturally persecute those who follow Christ and promote His teachings (to the point of killing Christians, as is happening in many parts of the world).

And You Think You've Got It Rough

To get a little more "up close and personal" with Paul and learn about the brutal experiences Paul endured, read his "testimony" in 2 Corinthians 11:23-33.

You might be tempted to ask why Paul would consider the service of Christ to be an honor when it involves such hardship. Paul answers that question in his next sentence (1:25). God has commissioned him to reveal the answer to an age-old mystery. Here is the secret that Paul is privileged to disclose (drum roll, please): God's salvation is available to non-Jews! Okay, maybe that isn't earth-shattering news to you, but it was to many people living in the first century A.D.

During the times of the Old Testament, God worked through the Jews as His chosen people to reveal His existence and precepts to the world at large. Through the Jews God revealed His principles for living (the Ten Commandments) and His structure for worship (through symbolic sacrifices). The Jewish prophets announced God's plan for salvation through the Messiah (who would be of Jewish lineage). Do you see how the Jews could have assumed that Christ's salvation was intended exclusively for the Jews? But God's plan, from the outset, was to extend the gift of salvation to all of humanity—to the Jews *and* to the Gentiles (non-Jews).

The revelation of God's secret did not receive universal acceptance. Many people were opposed to Paul's message that salvation was available to everyone:

- Many of the Jews, even the Christian Jews, opposed it. They could not comprehend that the God of the Jews could also be the God of the Gentiles. They had centuries of worshiping God in their ancestry. They didn't think salvation should be extended to the pagan Gentiles who had persecuted the Jews during all of those years.

- And the gnostics rejected Paul's claim of salvation for everyone. They could never agree with the notion because, for them, the knowledge of God was an intellectual concept so complex and intricate that most people lacked the mental horsepower to approach God. They couldn't tolerate a faith system that allowed nonintellectuals to share in privileges they thought they alone deserved.

But Paul took pleasure in dispelling these false notions. That is why he was willing to work so tirelessly. He wanted people to realize the truth of Christ and to mature in that understanding.

The Characteristics of Faith Based on Truth (2:1-7)

When Paul talked about the privilege of laboring so intensely to preach the truth of the Gospel, he had the Christians in Colosse (and Laodicea) in mind. Even though he had never seen most of them, they were part of that group that he wanted to "present...to God, perfect in their relationship to Christ" (1:28).

What follows in this passage is Paul's goal and prayer for the Colossian Christians (and all Christians for that matter). Here he reveals the nature of a mature faith that is based on the truth of Christ:

1. Courageous Hearts

Although he uses the term "encouraged," Paul's meaning is different than our use of that word. He is not implying that they would be comforted, consoled, or supported. Rather, he wants them to have confidence to withstand difficulties and hardships.

2. A Fellowship Knit Together in Love

Handling tough circumstances is easier collectively as a body of Christians (a church) rather than individually. But only love can hold them together as a church. Paul talks a great deal about church governance and administration in other letters (for instance, 1 Timothy 3), but he omits any such discussion here. The organizational structure is meaningless if a church doesn't have a foundation of love.

3. Wisdom and Understanding

Paul uses three different Greek words as he describes how a Christian processes information about his or her faith. First, Christians should understand *(sunesis)* God's plan that life is found in Jesus Christ. This is an essential fact; without an understanding of it, you are operating outside of God's paradigm. Then Paul refers to knowledge *(gnosis)* and wisdom *(sophia)* that are found in Christ. These two terms have an important distinction: *gnosis* is the ability to gain insights as truth is revealed to us; *sophia* is the ability to comprehend truth so that it can be communicated to others. Notice the interesting progress of these three words. First we have to have an understanding of Christ. After we experience the reality of living in Him, we will have a better knowledge of truth. Further growth as a Christian will give us the wisdom to articulate that truth to others.

4. The Power to Resist Deceptive Teachings

A mature faith (based on understanding, knowledge, and wisdom) is exactly what the Colossians need to refute the false teaching of the gnostics. To anyone else, the philosophical arguments of the gnostics might be enticing or intellectually seductive, but a Christian with a firm grasp of the truth won't get suckered by them. (This same type of mature faith is what you'll need to resist specious arguments and to articulate the relevance of Christianity in your culture.)

5. The Power to Persist in Their Faith

Standing firm and persisting in truth against an onslaught of heresy is not easy. You'll make enemies in the process. You will grow weary. But realization of the truth should motivate Christians to remain steadfast.

6. A Life Rooted in Christ

Paul uses the analogy of a tree to explain how a Christian derives the essence of life from Christ. A tree's roots grow deeper and wider in the soil to provide nutrients to the tree; those embedded roots also provide stability for the tree. And so it is with a Christian and Jesus. Paul expects that we will grow roots of understanding, knowledge, and wisdom deep into Christ. By so doing, we'll receive the spiritual nourishment we need to live in obedience to Him, and we'll have the strength and stability to withstand the winds of false teaching.

7. Abundant Gratitude

Realization of what Christ has done for us and what He means to us produces an attitude of gratitude. It is the natural response.

---

*T*ime to *E*valuate

Now is a great time to make another evaluation on the condition of your spiritual life. Use Paul's checklist for the characteristics of a mature Christian. How many of these characteristics are present in your life?

Using the Truth to Spot Deception (2:8-23)

Having established Christ as the truth detector for a mature Christian, Paul now subjects the gnostic philosophy to a biblical polygraph examination. He covers many specifics, but the precepts of gnosticism discussed here fall into three categories. The test results are the same each time: They are all *lies!*

1. The Deception of Human Thinking (2:8-10)

Truth comes from God. Everything else comes from the faulty reasoning of humans or the evil ploys of Satan. Unless you are careful, you can be led astray by these erroneous philosophies and views. Oftentimes, these concocted opinions are presented as "additional truth." In other words, people take the truths contained in the Bible, and then they seek to add something to it. ("Yes, the Bible is true, but we have additional information that you need to know. Without it, you won't really have salvation.") *"Lie!"* says Paul. You are complete as a Christian by your union with Jesus Christ. Since He has all authority and all supremacy, you require nothing else.

2. The Deception of Rules and Regulations (2:11-18)

The Colossian heresy included the requirement of compliance with many of the Jewish rituals, such as circumcision. (Circumcision, instituted at the time of Abraham, served as a physical reminder that the Jews were God's chosen people.) The Jews also celebrated special feasts and holy days. While these traditions represent a rich Hebrew heritage, are they necessary components of salvation? *"No!"* according to the truth of the Gospel. The need and requirement for those rituals vanished when Christ was crucified on the cross. His work of salvation put to death our old nature, and we are free from those regulations by our new life in Christ.

3. The Deception of the Spirit World (2:18-19)

Angel worship was also a tenant of gnosticism. (Lacking the intellectualism to worship God, you had to settle for worshiping the lower emanations of Him.) But according to the truth of Christ, this concept is *"False!"* Paul does not deny the reality of the spirit world (both angels and demons), but they are nothing to be worshiped. People who promote such nonsense aren't connected to Christ.

Paul concludes his "truth quest" with a startling conclusion (2:20-23). These deceptive doctrines (despite their spiritual context and their intellectual appeal) are hollow and empty. They obviously don't change a person on the inside. They may compel an outward compliance to a certain set of standards, but they don't change the condition of a person's heart. The truth of Christ, however, is just the opposite. Christ changes a person from the inside out. Once a person's heart is in a correct relationship with God, the thinking processes change, and right thinking leads to right living. Consequently, Christianity is not about rules and regulations. It's about a relationship.

Following the precepts of the Colossian heresy would result in bondage (with all its rules and regulations). Following Christ brings freedom. The best choice becomes obvious when we analyze the options in the light of Christ's truth.

Don't Concede Your Freedom in Christ

Some people in Christian circles try to attach extra requirements onto the Christian life. Such a legalistic approach adds do's and don'ts to the Christian life. Certainly there are standards of conduct that are appropriate for anyone who claims the name of Christ. But salvation has no requirements other than faith in Christ. Don't let anyone saddle you with the bondage and baggage of man-made rituals.

Study the Word

1. Read 1 Peter 4:1-2,12-19. And reread Colossians 1:24-29. Why isn't Paul bothered by the tremendous suffering and hardship that he endures?

2. What is the great mystery that Paul has revealed? Why was this a secret for such a long time? Why would people be opposed to this information?

3. Christianity involves giving yourself to Christ and turning control over to Him. How does that result in freedom?

4. Obviously, you can't disregard every new teaching you hear as being heresy. As young Christians grow in their faith, they will encounter many new insights into biblical Christianity. That is part of the under-standing-knowledge-wisdom process. But how can you tell if a teaching that someone presents is just new to you or a concocted philosophy? What are some questions you should ask as part of the truth-finding analysis?

5. What do you consider to be the key verse from this passage of Colossians 1:24–2:23? Explain why that verse best represents the points Paul makes.

Paul's Familiar Format

If you've read several of Paul's epistles, you might be experiencing déjà vu. Colossians may be starting to seem somewhat familiar to you—similar to his other letters—and it has a good reason to. Paul often followed a familiar format in his letters:

- first, a personal greeting

- next, some deep theology

- then, tips for practical living

- finally, personal comments

And the themes of many of his letters overlap. In fact, the letters of Ephesians and Colossians share a striking similarity. (Of the 155 verses in Ephesians, 78 of them appear in substantially similar form in Colossians.)

Colossians is one of the best examples of Paul's standard format. We've covered the personal greeting and the deep theology. Now we're in the part where he is getting practical. In chapter 3 he will be giving some practical statements about how to live a righteous life. But, having just finished a tirade against the do's and don'ts of the Colossian heresy, don't expect Paul to tell you *what to do* as a Christian. Remember, outside behavior isn't what Christianity is all about. Rather, he'll talk about *what you should be thinking about*. Right thinking leads to correct behavior. If your mind is focused on Christ, then righteous living will automatically follow.

Chapter 12

Knowing the Implications
of Your New Life

Colossians 3:1-17

_A_s you read this next passage, you might think that Paul is dropping the arguments against the Colossian heresy. You may assume that he has exposed those fallacies, and now he can move on to more practical matters—like finding purpose and enjoyment from the Christian life. You are correct that he is moving to more practical issues of living the Christian life, but he hasn't finished deflating the premises of gnosticism. The gnostics wanted to downplay the significance of Christ; Paul, on the other hand, says that the Christian life only works if Christ is in the center of it. If you've ever wondered why your life seems less fulfilling than you expected it would be as a Christian, then this next passage is for you.

You've Got a New Life with Christ (3:1-4)

Your understanding of this passage will be enhanced if you have a mental picture of baptism. Baptism for Christians in the first century A.D. followed the pattern of Christ's baptism—the convert entered the river or lake, was lowered below the surface of the water, and rose up out of the water. It was nothing fancy—just dunk down and pop back up.

The ordinance of baptism is basically a public profession of a Christian's faith. Of course, a person could just make a vocal statement of this fact, but the great symbolism of baptism would be lost. Going below the water represents the death of our old sinful nature; rising out of the water represents our new life in Christ.

Back in Colossians 2:20, Paul referred to our dying with Christ. Now in 3:1, he begins with a reference to being "raised to new life with Christ." Based on these references, Bible scholars are convinced that Paul had the ordinance of baptism in mind as he wrote this passage. They are equally sure that his terminology would have brought baptism to the mind of his Colossian readers. With that picture in your mind, look at the points he makes about our new life as Christians:

1. Raised to a New Life with Christ

Sometime in the future, at the return of Christ, all Christians will receive a new resurrection body. This will happen to the Christians living at that time as well as all the Christians who physically died prior to that event. (See Romans 8:11 and 1 Corinthians 15:22-23,50-55 for more about this.) But Paul isn't referring to this future resurrection. Notice that he talks in the past tense. We already "have been raised to new life with Christ" (3:1).

Thus he is talking about our identification with Christ's death, burial, and resurrection. Because we are in Christ, we *already* have this new life.

2. A New Perspective

Since we have a new life with citizenship in heaven, our mindset shouldn't be fixed on earthly matters. Instead, we should operate under a new, spiritual paradigm. Our focus should be on spiritual matters; our perspective should be eternal rather than temporal.

Should We Be So Heavenly Minded That We're No Earthly Good?

Paul is saying that we should be thinking with a heavenly mind-set rather than being bogged down with the trivialities of an earthly existence. Is he suggesting that we should disengage from all of life's entanglements and move to a mountaintop to contemplate spiritual matters? Not hardly. That might be good for a weekend church retreat, but Paul is expecting that the Colossians keep working at their jobs and be contributing members of society. Notice that he says, "Do not think *only* about things down here" (3:2). And in a few verses, he'll be talking about the ethical principles of relationships for bosses and employees. So Paul expects that you'll still give attention to the realities of life (such as mortgage payments and work schedules). He just expects that you move those down on your priority list and put matters of eternal significance at the top.

3. Hidden with Christ in God

Paul is not suggesting that our Christian faith should be camouflaged so no one notices it. He is making a play on words that his Greek audience would understand.

When a person died, the Greeks said that the person was "hidden in the earth" (in other words, the earth is now the dwelling place of the person). When Christians identify with Christ and declare the death of their old nature, they become "hidden with Christ in God" (3:4). We dwell in God side by side with Christ.

4. Christ Is Our Real Life

Christ is not just an important part of life. For the Christian, He is life itself. (You already saw Paul make this point in Philippians 1:21.)

Let What's Dead Stay Dead (3:5-11)

Living the Christian life is not easy. It is not just "believe in Christ and let God do the rest." Sanctification (the process of becoming more Christlike) requires us to be proactive. In the positive sense, Paul has just said that we need to focus our thoughts on God; we should be thinking of things that are moral, pure, and true. In the negative sense, we need to rid our mind of things that are just the opposite.

Our old nature died when we accepted Christ as Savior. We have been raised to a new life. But we bring that old nature back to life when we entertain thoughts that are earthly instead of heavenly. Here is where Paul gets brutal. He says we are to kill any inappropriate thoughts. He doesn't delicately suggest that we should think about such things with less frequency. He tells us to put them to death. Do it abruptly and with finality.

Notice that Paul doesn't have to describe a long list of behavior and conduct. He isn't making a new Ten Commandments. Instead, he goes to the root of all sinful actions—our thoughts. He does so in two separate lists.

1. Perverted Passions (3:5)

These are the "it's all about me" sinful thoughts because they are centered in selfishness. At their core, the sin is idolatry because we have given these desires that priority in our life that Christ deserves. Whether these vices stay within the mind or culminate in external behavior, the result is the same: They are evil.

2. Hostile Thoughts Toward Other People (3:9-9)

Here Paul changes the metaphor. He says that we are to "take off" or "get rid" of this animosity. The picture goes back to baptism. People who were baptized would drop their dusty outer garment on the ground as they walked into the water. After they emerged from the water, they received a white robe to wear, symbolizing their new life. Paul knows that people tend to harbor bitterness toward each other. We keep it in our minds and won't let go of it. But how can we be focusing on God when we're angry toward other people and strategizing ways to retaliate against them? Paul wants us to drop those thoughts on the ground and walk away from them.

Our new nature is like that white robe that people wore after baptism. In the new life, Christ is all that matters. We leave behind selfish thoughts; we throw off hostility toward other people. Any external distinctions and barriers that typically divide people are irrelevant:

- Racial distinctions (Greek or Jew) don't matter.

- Religious distinctions (circumcised or uncircumcised) don't matter.

- Cultural distinctions (civilized or barbarian, such as the wild and savage Scythian nomads) don't matter.

- Societal distinctions (slave or free) don't matter.

The only thing that matters is Christ.

Keeping the Old Nature Dead and Buried

Does Paul expect that we can do this by our own initiative and in our own power? Absolutely not. Even though our old nature is dead, we aren't capable of walking away and letting that corpse rot in the ground. When temptation comes our way, we dig up our old nature, give it CPR, and bring it back to the party. Let's face it. We do a poor job at keeping that old nature in the coffin. Paul knows that. He struggled with the same problems (see Romans 7:14-25).

Christians are not do-it-yourselfers who depend solely on a positive mental attitude. Left to our own resources, we're powerless. But that is exactly why God gave us a supernatural power source: The Holy Spirit. Paul explained this in his letter to the Romans:

So, dear brothers and sisters, you have no obligation whatsoever to do what your sinful nature urges you to do. For if you keep on following it, you will perish. But if through the power of the Holy Spirit *you turn from it and its evil deeds, you will live* (Romans 8:12-13, emphasis added).

There's the not-so-secret solution to our struggles with the old nature. We need to let the Holy Spirit have full control of our lives. And that happens only as we continue to stay focused on Christ and not on the baggage and temptations of the world.

Live for Jesus (3:12-17)

Going back to the white robe analogy, Paul next states that we, as Christians, should *put on* some qualities in our new life. Again, notice that he isn't giving us a checklist of behaviors with which we must comply on a constant basis. He is talking about attitudes—qualities of our hearts—that should arise naturally from our transformed lives (3:12-15).

ℱruit of the 𝒮pirit

This passage isn't the only place in which Paul discusses the Christlike qualities that should be evident in the life of a believer. In Galatians 5:22-23, Paul discusses the "fruit of the Spirit." Immediately prior to those verses, he explained that the qualities of your old nature would only be pushed out of your life as you fill your life with the character traits that come from the Holy Spirit:

So I advise you to live according to your new life in the Holy Spirit. Then you won't be doing what your sinful nature craves. The old sinful nature loves to do evil, which is just opposite from what the Holy Spirit wants. And the Spirit gives us desires that are opposite from what the sinful nature desires. These two forces are constantly fighting each other, and your choices are never free from this conflict. But when you are directed by the Holy Spirit, you are no longer subject to the law (Galatians 5:16-18).

Do you struggle with temptation? Do you find yourself harboring thoughts and attitudes that you know are dishonoring to God? Have you tried—unsuccessfully—to maintain a mental focus on Christ? You aren't alone. Paul knew that the Colossian Christians were struggling with the same issues. Getting rid of the wrong thoughts wasn't enough; he encourages them to fill their minds with those things that were moral, pure, and true.

Although some analogy to taking out the trash could be made, this isn't something that can be done once a week. It is a continual process. That's why Paul concludes this passage with an imperative in 3:16 that conveys the constant process of transformed thinking:

- Read and memorize the words of Christ to renew your heart and mind.

- Discuss biblical principles with each other so that you may grow in spiritual maturity.

- Worship together in songs that direct your gratitude to God.

The end result of these disciplines will be a life that reflects Christ in "whatever you do or say" (3:17).

■ ■ ■

Study the Word

1. Read Romans 6:1-14 and 7:4-6. What do these passages explain about the death of the old nature and our new life in Christ?

2. Explain how we can "put to death" and "get rid of" thoughts and attitudes that are inconsistent with a Christlike life.

3. Review the list of characteristics that Paul says we should put on in Colossians 3:12-15. Explain how each one reflects Christ's character and promotes building loving relationships.

4. How does singing songs of worship fit into the points that Paul makes in this passage?

5. Why does Paul say that love is the "most important piece of clothing" that we can put on (3:14)?

It's All About Relationships

As we begin the last chapter of our study of Colossians, perhaps a recap is in order.

> *Colossians 1:* We should know that Christ has supremacy and is preeminent in all things.

> *Colossians 2:* Our knowledge of Christ can be used to detect false teachings that don't match what we know to be true about Him.

> *Colossians 3:* Our knowledge of Christ should prompt us to reject our old nature and live according to the new life that He has secured for us.

That's wonderful in theory, isn't it? But how does it play out in your living room, on the job, and in your neighbor's yard? Those are fair and practical questions, and Paul is going to answer them.

The Christian life is all about relationships: yours with Christ, and yours with other people. In typical fashion, Paul has laid out the underlying theology before he gets to the practical tips of day-to-day living.

You're also about to read Paul's sign-off to his Colossian letter. Don't skip what you might otherwise think is just a list of names. Paul gives us clues about his relationship with each person. You'll be able to tell why Paul can speak with authority about relationships. He was a master of them because he allowed Christ to be the Master of his life.

Chapter 13

Knowing the Practicalities of Your Faith

Colossians 3:18–4:18

What's Ahead

- ☐ Family Life (3:18-21)

- ☐ Work Life (3:22–4:1)

- ☐ Prayer Life (4:2-4)

- ☐ Public Life (4:5-6)

- ☐ Final Greetings (4:7-18)

*R*emember where we left off in the last chapter. Paul has just finished reviewing the Christlike character qualities that we should put on. Now we need to take those qualities out for a test drive and see how they really work. Reading and talking about those traits theoretically is one thing. But Paul knew the Colossians weren't living theoretical lives, so he takes these characteristics for a spin where he knows the rubber will meet the road.

Family Life (3:18-21)

Paul's great desire for the Colossians is that they be authentic Christians. The very best place to test the authenticity of your new life is in your own household. That is where people know you the best. We can be on our best behavior when we're away from home, but we usually drop our guard the moment we walk through the garage door into the kitchen. So Paul uses this context to give some practical guidelines to show how we can incorporate the Christian traits of Colossians 3:12-15 into our everyday lives. He focuses on the dynamics of relationships between (1) husbands and wives, and (2) parents and children.

Husbands and Wives (3:18-19)

Notice the reciprocal relationship between the spouses. It is not one-sided in favor of the husband. This was radical thinking for the first century A.D. Both the Hebrew and Greek cultures had a low opinion of women. Instead of valuing women as individuals, the prevailing customs denigrated them and assigned them to roles of sexual gratification, procreation, child raising, and household tasks. They often had no more dignity than cattle or other property the husband owned. Against this cultural setting, Paul places the wife and the husband on equal footing. Both have value as individuals before God, and both play a key role in the marriage relationship.

Paul does not disparage the role of the wife by saying that she alone should practice submission. Submission is a character trait that all Christians should have—male and female alike:

> Submit to one another out of reverence for Christ (Ephesians 5:21).

Paul taught that the husband has leadership in the home (Ephesians 5:23), but his discussions of marriage always suggest that it is to be a cooperative partnership. Submission by the wife does not mean abject subservience to the dictates of a totalitarian husband (as was the custom for the Greeks). Rather, the wife has the privilege to accept (submit to) the loving leadership of the husband. Don't miss that key word for the husband's role: *love*. It goes way beyond the notion of romantic love. Paul sets the standard for self-sacrificial love in Ephesians 5:25:

> *And you husbands must love your wives with the same love Christ showed the church.*

Parents and Children (3:20-21)

That same reciprocal relationship of submission and love pertains to the parent-child relationship. Paul's comments are culturally radical here as well. The Colossians' society gave children less value than women. Kids were expected to act in strict compliance with their father's dictates. Disobedience included severe corporal punishment. Asking a child to show respect for a father wasn't anything new. But Paul put a twist on it. He was asking children to honor their fathers, not because it was required but because it was an appropriate response to the father's leadership role. (This is consistent with Paul's emphasis on proper attitudes as the motivation for actions.) His comments to fathers is even more socially controversial. He clearly showed that discipline was not within the father's arbitrary domain. Instead, discipline was put in the context of nurturing instruction necessary to develop the child according to God's principles. The parental goal becomes *instruction,* and discipline—

along with encouragement—are tools to be administered to accomplish the objective.

$\mathscr{A}$ Contemporary $\mathscr{E}$quivalent

Slaves often lived in their master's household during the first century A.D. Paul naturally includes them in discussions of the spousal and parent-child relationships.

The closest contemporary equivalent to the master-servant relationship is that of boss and employee. As you read Colossians 3:22–4:1, you can replace *master* with *employer* and substitute *employee* for *slave*.

Work Life (3:22–4:1)

If you are looking for a standard for Christian business ethics, you will be well served to remember the verse regarding all relationships that immediately precedes this passage of Colossians 3:18–4:1:

> *And whatever you do or say, let it be as a representative of the Lord Jesus* (Colossians 3:17).

With that standard in mind, we shouldn't be surprised that Paul tells the slaves to be conscientious workers and the masters to be fair and kindhearted. There are two bits of radical thought in the passage:

An Inheritance in Heaven

In that society, slaves could not own property. (They were property themselves, so they could not legally own anything.) As slaves, they were even disqualified from inheriting property. Perhaps that is why Paul reminds them that their real Master is Christ and that they have an inheritance coming from the Lord—an eternal benefit plan. He tries to get them to focus on the eternal perspective (a heavenly mind-set that he talked about in Colossians 3:2) by getting them to realize that Christ is their real Master. For His sake they should work diligently for their earthly masters.

A Master in Heaven

The masters were the ultimate bosses. They were accountable to no one. No Fair Employment Commissions or labor unions existed to protect the slaves. A master could do with his slaves as he pleased because he had no master above him. However, as Paul explains, this is not the case with the Christian masters. They have a Master—Christ—to whom they are accountable. They should consider that their business ventures are really God's businesses. They are just the middle managers and stewards of what really belongs to God. As such, they need to operate their businesses—and treat their slaves—with the dignity that God ascribes to those individuals.

You may fit into this passage in one way or the other. If you are someone's employee, your identity with Christ should compel you to be the best employee in the workforce. Don't complain or cut corners. Consider Christ to be your boss, and work hard for His sake and pleasure. Conversely, if you are an employer, then realize that Christ is the owner of your business and that you work for Him. In your role as the resident manager of the operation, treat each employee with the same personal interest that your Boss has for them.

Prayer Life (4:2-4)

In talking about personal relationships, Paul can't resist the urge to mention the daily relationship that you should establish with God in prayer. With Paul, daily prayer is the daily duty and privilege of each believer.

Paul asks that they pray for him. Read this request carefully. He isn't asking for prayers from a selfish perspective. His request is really for prayers for his ministry. Rather than asking for comforts or conveniences (and the list of these from someone in prison could be very long), Paul simply asks for more strength and more opportunity to spread the Gospel. We should take a clue from this. As we pray for ourselves and for others, are we focused more on *things* than we should be? Or are our prayers like Paul's, reflecting the point of Colossians 3:11 that "Christ is all that matters."

Public Life (4:5-6)

Paul has just asked for prayers in his efforts to spread the Gospel. To avoid any misconception that the task of evangelism is his alone, he reminds the Colossians that they too are to be testimonies for Christ to the unbelievers in their sphere of influence. Notice the implications of these two verses:

- Paul does not believe that our lives should be insulated from contact with non-Christians. Life might be easier for us if we only socialized and did business with other believers, but Jesus never intended that. He wants us in the world (John 17:18). We need to be engaged in activities with the people of our communities, not isolated from them in a holy cocoon.

- We must live in such a manner that non-Christians are attracted to us. That shouldn't be a problem if

the Holy Spirit has control in our lives and produces the characteristics of Colossians 3:12-14.

- We should be looking for opportunities to share
  our experience with Christ. This will require tact
  and sensitivity on our part.

- We must be ready to give an answer about our
  faith when we are asked about it. Our words must
  be chosen carefully and spoken graciously. As
  Peter said:

  And if you are asked about your Christian hope,
  always be ready to explain it. But you must do
  this in a gentle and respectful way (1 Peter
  3:15-16).

Final Greetings (4:7-18)

Paul seems to have three purposes in mind as he
writes Colossians. They aren't equal in importance, and
he saved the least for the last. As you already know, his
primary purpose was to show the deity and supremacy
of Christ in the face of the Colossian heresy. A related
purpose, although somewhat less urgent, was his usual
overriding theme of leading believers into a deeper spiritual maturity. Now, as he closes his letter, he'll touch
upon the last and probably least important of his
themes: informing the Colossians of his personal situation. Two members of the Colossian church, Tychicus
and Onesimus, will deliver Paul's status report. They will
also be the messengers who hand-carry Paul's letter to
the church.

Paul mentions six men who want their greetings con-
veyed to the Colossian Christians:

- Three are Jewish men who are part of Paul's support team in prison: Aristarchus, Mark, and Justus.

- Three are Gentiles who are with Paul as well: Epaphras (who came from Colosse and was apparently staying with Paul a little longer), Luke the physician, and Demas.

The false teaching of the gnostics was not limited to the city of Colosse. It had infected the entire Lycus Valley. For that reason, Paul wanted this letter (with its refutation of the Colossian heresy) to be passed along to the Christians in Laodicea. Then in 4:16-17, we find two mysteries for which scholars have no definitive answers:

- Paul mentions that he wrote a letter to the Laodiceans that should be read by the Colossians. Some scholars think that the letter referred to is our Ephesians; others think it may be Philemon. The best guess seems to be that the letter was lost.

- Not much is known about Archippus or the nature of his work. No one knows what prompted Paul to mention him at this point in the letter.

Although most of the letter was probably transcribed by someone while Paul dictated it, he adds a personal touch by signing off in his own handwriting. "Remember my chains" is a cryptic request to be upheld in their prayers as he continues to minister even while in prison.

Don't let the anticlimactic ending of this letter distract you from the impact of the epistle's message: Your knowledge of the supremacy and preeminence of Christ is all you need to refute false teaching and enjoy new life. With the confidence of that knowledge, the joy of the Christian life is yours!

■ ▨ ▣

Study the Word

1. Review the list of "new life" character traits in Colossians 3:12-15. In what way are a few of these demonstrated in your household?

2. Explain the reciprocal relationships that Paul envisions between husbands and wives. Explain the attitudes a Christian wife should exhibit (without using the words *submit* or *submission*).

3. How would you respond to a non-Christian friend who said, "Christians seem so judgmental and intolerant. You don't seem that way. How can you buy into that Christianity stuff?"

4. What does Paul mean when he writes, "devote your-
    self to prayer"?

5. Summarize what you consider to be the main points
    of Paul's letter to the Colossians.

Dig Deeper

*I*f you would like to dig deeper into the background of Philippians or Colossians, we can recommend some great books:

Commentaries

William Barclay has written a great Bible commentary set. In a single volume (published by Westminster Press) you can find his *Letters to the Philippians, Colossians and Thessalonians*. Barclay is known for great scholarship and readability.

Another commentary set, with basically a verse-by-verse analysis, is the *Tyndale New Testament Commentaries*. You don't have to buy the entire set. You can select Philippians (volume 11) by Ralph P. Martin, or Colossians and Philemon (volume 12) by N.T. Wright.

Dr. Roy L. Laurin wrote the Life commentary set. The two volumes that you'll be interested in are *Philippians: Where Life Advances* and *Colossians: Where Life is Established*. This set is currently out of print, but you can find used copies on the Internet.

Another commentary set, a bit on the more scholarly side, is the *New Testament Commentary* by William Hendriksen and Simon J. Kistemaker. This is a 12-volume set, but Philippians, Colossians, and Philemon are contained in a single volume.

An excellent and detailed set is *The New International Commentary on the New Testament*. The volume on Philippians was written by Gordon D. Fee, and the volume on Ephesians, Colossians, and Philemon was written by F.F. Bruce.

We also enjoy using *The IVP Bible Background Commentary* (New Testament) by Craig S. Keener. This book focuses on the cultural background of the Bible text.

General Bible Study Helps

Do you wonder how Philippians and Colossians fit into the flow of the entire Bible? You might want to read *Knowing the Bible 101* by us (Bruce Bickel and Stan Jantz). Like the other books in the Christianity 101 series, it is designed to be reader-friendly.

Of course, no book is as good as reading the Bible itself. If you want to be a real student of the Bible, we're glad to recommend *How to Study the Bible* by Kay Arthur. Kay is a noted Bible teacher and a gracious lady, but she won't cut you any slack. You'll be doing the work yourself.

A Word About Translations

Whenever we quoted Scripture in this study, we used the New Living Translation. We like the way this translation flows. It uses a translation method referred to as "dynamic equivalence" which means the Bible was translated from the original texts on a "thought for thought" basis. (The New International Version is also a "dynamic equivalence" translation.) Other Bible translations, such as the New American Standard, are just as accurate but use a "word for word" approach. The important thing is for you to use a Bible that you'll actually read. You might even prefer a Bible paraphrase, such as *The Living Bible* or *The Message*, for your devotional reading.

The authors of this book would enjoy hearing from you. Contact them with your questions, comments, or to schedule them to speak at an event:

Twelve Two Media Group
P.O. Box 25997
Fresno CA 93729-5997

Email: info@TwelveTwoMedia.com
Website: www.TwelveTwoMedia.com

Exclusive Online Feature

Here's a Bible study feature you're really going to like! Simply go online at:

www.christianity101online.com

There you'll find a website designed exclusively for users of the Christianity 101 Bible Studies series. When you log on to the site, just click on the book you are studying, and you will discover additional information, resources, and helps, including...

- *Background Material*—We can't put everything in this Bible study, so this online section includes more material, such as historical, geographical, theological, and biographical information.

- *More Questions*—Do you need more questions for your Bible study? Here are additional questions for each chapter. Bible study leaders will find this especially helpful.

- *Answers to Your Questions*—Do you have a question about something in your Bible study? Post your question and an "online scholar" will respond.

- *FAQs*—In this section are answers to some of the more frequently asked questions about the book you are studying.

What are you waiting for? Go online and become a part of the Christianity 101 community!

Christianity 101™ Bible Studies

Genesis: Discovering God's Answers to Life's Ultimate Questions

What did God have in mind when He started this world? What happened to His perfect design? Join Bruce & Stan in this exciting survey, and learn how God's record of ancient times impacts *our* time.

John: Encountering Christ in a Life-Changing Way

John records how Jesus changed the lives of everyone He met. Bruce and Stan's fresh approach to these narratives will help you have your own personal, life-changing encounter with Jesus, the Son of God.

Romans: Understanding God's Grace and Power

Paul's letter to the church in Rome is his clearest explanation and application of the Good News. This fresh study of Romans assures you that the Gospel is God's answer to every human need.

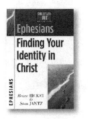

Ephesians: Finding Your Identity in Christ

This inviting little guide to the book of Ephesians gets straight to the heart of Paul's teaching on the believer's identity in Christ: We belong to Christ, the Holy Spirit is our guarantee, and we can share in God's power.

Philippians/Colossians: Experiencing the Joy of Knowing Christ

This new 13-week study of two of Paul's most intimate letters inspires you to know Christ more intimately and maintain your passion and vision. It is filled with helpful background information, up-to-date applications, and penetrating, open-ended questions.

Revelation: Unlocking the Mysteries of the End Times

Just what is really going to happen? In this fascinating look at the apostle John's prophecy, Bruce and Stan demonstrate why—when God's involved—the end of the world is something to look forward to.

Knowing the Bible 101

A fresh approach to making Christianity understandable—even the hard parts! This user-friendly book relies on humor, insights, and relevant examples that will inspire you not only to make sense of Scripture but to *enjoy* Bible study.

Creation & Evolution 101

With their distinctively winsome style, Bruce and Stan explore the essentials of creation and evolution and offer fascinating evidence of God's hand at work. Perfect for individual or group use.

Bruce & Stan's *Guide Series:*

Bruce & Stan's® Guide to Bible Prophecy

Dealing with prophecy and end times in their witty, down-to-earth way, Bruce and Stan offer the Bible's answers to readers' big questions. Is the end really near? Who is the Antichrist? What is the Rapture?

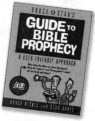

Bruce & Stan's® Guide to Cults, Religions, and Spiritual Beliefs

"Here is our purpose, plain and simple: to provide an understandable overview of predominant religions and spiritual beliefs (with a little sense of humor thrown in along the way)." Clear explanations help readers understand the core issues of more than a dozen religions.

Bruce & Stan's® Guide to God

This fresh, user-friendly guide to the Christian life is designed to help new believers get started or recharge the batteries of believers of any age. Humorous subtitles, memorable icons, and learning aids present even difficult concepts in a simple way. Perfect for personal use or group study.